THE BONNIE CODE

THE BONNIE CODE

A True Story

One Girl's Battle With Mitochondrial Disease,
Using Joy As Her Armor

By Thomas Wayne Sanders

XULON PRESS ELITE

Xulon Press Elite
2301 Lucien Way #415
Maitland, FL 32751
407.339.4217
www.xulonpress.com

Unless otherwise indicated, Scripture quotations taken from the New King James Version (NKJV). Copyright © 1982 by Thomas Nelson, Inc. Used by permission. All rights reserved.

Scripture quotations taken from the Holy Bible, New Living Translation (NLT). Copyright ©1996, 2004, 2007 by Tyndale House Foundation. Used by permission of Tyndale House Publishers, Inc.

Printed in the United States of America.

ISBN-13: 978-1-6312-9367-2

Acknowledgements

To my wife, Kimberly, for believing that someday I would finally finish this.

To the Codier family for allowing me into their lives.

To my mother for introducing me to Jesus.

To my friend, Steve Brown, for his constant support on the project, especially for sharing with me the wisdom that the perfect book had never been written—and I wasn't going to write it, either.

To the pastors, staff, and volunteers at all Redemption Church locations, where the love of Christ, volunteerism, and compassion are evident every day.

To the other Bonnie-sitters, whose lives were also blessed by Bonnie Codier.

And, finally, to Bonnie—for her joy, laughter, and incredible friendship.

Bonnie Codier at ten years old

TABLE OF CONTENTS

INTRODUCTION

I n 2011, I met Bonnie Codier and her family after answering an email from a member of my church's Compassion Ministry team. They were looking for a Bonnie-sitter. Leaving Bonnie's home after that first visit, I sat in quiet retrospection in my vehicle for a few minutes. As I drove away, I thought to myself, I have to tell the story of this girl and the joy that she shares in the midst of her constant suffering.

Bonnie asked me several times over the years, as we sat together visiting, "Why do you think God brought us together? Aren't we an odd pair?" Usually, we'd simply laugh and shake our heads, knowing for sure He had a reason. We just didn't know what it was yet.

I commented to Bonnie a few times during our four years of conversations that it did seem strange the Lord brought us together—her, a young, very intelligent girl in her twenties, and me, an old guy about fifty that didn't know anything. She always got a kick out of that, making sure to tell me that I wasn't old, which is probably why I said it to her in the first place. Come to think of it, I don't believe she ever refuted that I didn't know anything. Hmm. Bonnie, you little rascal.

My hope as you read this story is three-fold:

1. That you meet Bonnie and are touched by her attitude about the life she was handed and that you realize the source of her joy and make it a part of your life or experience it more deeply

2. That by using personal experiences to compare my relatively healthy body to her afflicted body—her twenty-four seven physical struggles, discomfort, and pain—I don't detract from her story, but instead help make the point that no matter our physical condition, we can help others greatly if we simply make up our mind to do so and act on those decisions

3. That you learn more about mitochondrial disease, or Mito, through reading this story

Hopefully, Bonnie's story will bring Mito more to the forefront of medicine, providing those that battle this very challenging and mysterious disease on a daily basis and their loved ones better treatment and maybe even one day a cure. It is a battle.

Thankfully,
Tom Sanders

1

Exploring the Depths

"Have you explored the springs from which the seas come? Have you explored their depths?" **Job 38:16** (New Living Translation)

At seventy feet below the surface of the water, all was beautifully silent. Even with the relatively limited visibility of the warm Gulf of Mexico water in June, the ocean and its inhabitants were, no pun intended, breathtaking. My one and only favorite daughter, Korey, and I were enjoying the Sand Dollar Artificial Reef near Destin, Florida, during a family visit to the area. We were part of a fourteen-person boat dive, including our dive guides. Along with my brother, Phil, we were the only scuba-certified members of the family and had decided to take a day to check out God's underwater creatures.

I need to mention that Korey was both my one and only—and my favorite daughter—because that's how I've referred to her in person since I divorced her mother when she was ten years young.

Korey and I had just completed a cursory underwater evaluation of the Mohawk Chief, a crusty old ninety-three foot tugboat intentionally sunk on June 23, 2003. The colorful fish, plant life, and other spunky creatures appeared to be quite thankful that this particular ship had been laid softly in that precise spot. After we reached the bottom of the reef area, we checked out the vessel briefly, then circled away from the group to see what additional creatures we could find. I noticed that we couldn't see any of the other divers, including my brother, who had teamed up with another diver to forge their own adventure. No worries. We had ample air and knew they weren't too far away, simply that visibility was limited to only forty feet or so that day in the warm water of the Gulf.

We planned our dive to be about forty-five minutes and we continually checked our dive computers and communicated by hand signals, monitoring the remaining air in our tanks. I was thoroughly proud of Korey, twenty years old, for taking the initiative and the time to get the necessary certification to take these scuba adventures with me. We'd only been diving together once prior to this trip a couple of years earlier, and some pesky allergies of mine shortened our dives as we weaved through the kelp in the cool waters off Catalina Island, California, that day.

I didn't know, but as the time came to begin the ascent to the surface of the Gulf, Korey was suffering from a painful headache. If I'd known it earlier, I would have motioned for her to stop skip breathing, a technique of briefly holding your breath between inhales and exhales, and probably what she was doing. If you've never been scuba diving, you may wonder why someone would do this. However, once you see the beauty and tranquility of the ocean depths, it's easy to change the cadence of your breathing unknowingly. Some divers may intentionally use skip breathing to conserve air in their scuba tank and make the dive last longer. Although this may seem to make sense—and I'm sure Korey wasn't doing it on purpose—the practice is considered a very dangerous idea for any scuba enthusiast, as it has the opposite effect, causing an abundance of carbon dioxide to build in the blood. This condition, called hypercapnia, can cause drowsiness, headaches, shortness of breath, and muscular tremors and can be a dangerous scenario, whether diving or not.

Korey and I began rising slowly with small puffs of air into our buoyancy control vests, initiated by the thumb click of a button, still within reach of each other. I took the first look upward toward the surface and, in controlled horror, looked back at Korey's face. She apparently hadn't looked upward yet, because her eyeballs were still normal-sized.

A massive bloom of four-inch-wide jellyfish covered the entire upper thirty feet or so of the ocean. One floated every square foot or two as far around us as we could see in every direction. The piercing June sunlight from above illuminated the thousands upon thousands of jellyfish tendrils, creating an even more eerie view upward. We continued to ascend slowly. For the safety of our lungs, we couldn't rise too quickly to the surface.

Thoughts quickly raced through my head about swimming around the jellyfish cloud. But needing to balance the remaining air level in our tanks and not knowing the size of this group of beautiful creatures, I quickly decided that we would have to try and float upward, directly through them. Recognizing that these weren't one of the more dangerous species of jellyfish, I felt my one and only sigh of relief leave my body as a slow trail of bubbles, weaving their way silently and harmlessly between, around, and through the jellyfish tendrils and toward the surface. After a safety stop, Korey and I reached thirty-five feet and began to feel the stings.

In retrospect, I may have confused my hand signals and, instead of reminding Korey to stay calm, sent the silent directive to bolt as fast as humanly possible to the surface, because that is what my one and only favorite daughter tried to do. Multiple jellyfish were stinging us now. Their almost invisible tendrils wrapped around the right side of my face, my ear, and my neck. One was taking a joy ride on the inside of my right elbow, sending a loud and clear message that it was there to stay. Thankfully, within a second and before my daughter could get out of range, I kicked my fins and grabbed one of her ankles, pulling her violently back down to me. The next several seconds seemed like five minutes, as we screamed into our face masks, new stings all over our bodies, and quickly began using the remaining air in our tanks.

During all this havoc, my eyes frantically scanned the water above us for any sign of a boat. We saw no other divers until we finally broke the water's surface, the jellyfish still stinging. I immediately waved to the dive guides on the boat, approximately one hundred and fifty feet away. One guide didn't need my hand signal to process the situation. He'd already heard Korey's screams as she exploded out of the water. In one motion, he grabbed a boogie board and lunged off the bow of the boat, no doubt setting the fifty-meter freestyle record getting to us, as we began swimming toward him and away from the electric cloud.

Within a few minutes, we made it safely to the boat, the guide receiving a few stings himself. Korey's head wasn't well, but it appeared that her lungs had remained healthy, which was my main concern. We were apparently the only dive team with a story worth telling, based on the comments of the number of divers gathered around us. We noticed red welts elevating all over our skin, and Korey wished she hadn't decided to wear loose shorts on this particular dive.

The warm ocean breeze blew in our faces as the diesel engines cranked up and we began cruising back toward the Florida shoreline, the air drying our hair in comical shapes. I could only think, now that we were safe, of how beautiful those jellyfish were, simply floating there, not bothering anyone until we swam through them, no doubt irritating them.

The glaring sun bought me back to reality as I glanced over to my daughter, who felt somewhat better now that she was breathing deeply and the ibuprofen had kicked in. I was sure she was happy that we were finished with the water for the day. I closed my eyes for a moment, thanking the Lord that we made it through that ordeal without a noticeable injury and that we were blessed with the health and opportunity to do something like exploring the ocean depths. As the boat engines slowed and we coasted toward the dock, still breathing diesel fuel, my thoughts turned to someone who didn't have the health or the opportunity to experience this blessing of scuba—my friend, Bonnie Belle. I'd like to introduce you to her now. What better way to do so, than in her own words?

Bonnie's Journal Entry #1, September 24

Hi all,

I've been trying to get this update written for over three days now, but I've just been so exhausted I haven't been able to get myself to do it, so I apologize for the delay.

Since this likely will be the last update prior to having surgery (unless something changes at the last minute), I decided to decorate with a birthday theme, since my birthday is coming up on the

4th, and I definitely don't think I'll be up for changing the graphics and writing updates right after surgery.

I had the venogram last Monday, and it basically showed that my left arm is completely unusable (which was news but made sense since that's the arm I've had clots in before), and the interventional radiologist thought that it looked like I had an open vein on my right side. Given that I've had trouble with that side in the past (where it looked open, until they tried to thread a PICC and were unable to do so), so we're going to give it a try and hope it's successful this time.

We haven't talked with anesthesia yet, and we absolutely <u>have to</u> prior to the day of surgery. It's crucial that we can get with someone who is understanding and receptive (so many just want to ignore you and do things "their way"), since things are going to get really squirrely if the anesthesia is not done correctly for someone with Mito (who metabolizes things differently than most patients). We also already began the process of taking me off Coumadin and will start those lovely* lovenox injections tomorrow (*sarcasm).

So that's the deal as of right now. We still need to talk with infectious disease about a few things and, of course, if my body doesn't hold out until then I'd have to go in right away and do all the procedures separately. I'm trying not to get too anxious too far ahead of time. It'd be nice to avoid any nervousness altogether, but I don't know if that's doable. For the average person, these procedures wouldn't be too big of a deal, but given the Mito, the combination of multiple procedures, the anesthesia issues, and the fact that I've been dealing with an ongoing bacteremia for over 1.5 months all make for a much more complicated scenario. Plus, I haven't done this kind of thing in about 5.5 years, so I think some apprehension is normal. Also, I won't be sedated at all for the PICC placement (which usually people are), and given the past issues with trying to get one in, I'm not super excited to be wide awake for that experience (done it before and know the unpleasantness).

I think we are definitely going to have to push back my birthday celebration, as this year is a big deal, since I will be turning 30. I didn't know if I would make it to see my 30th year, so I am so grateful to be so close. I would love to make it further into my 30s—that's my goal, but what I had hoped would be a big celebration will now have to be postponed, since I will definitely still be trying to recover.

Thanks so much for your prayers. Please be praying not just for the surgery itself (and all the various components of the multiple things that will be happening), but also for my heart and for my parents, that we wouldn't be too anxious and be able to just rest peacefully in God's care ... though I think we are already dealing with some nerves. Thank you also for any notes left in the guestbook. ☺

Love and Hugs to You All,

Bonnie ☺

2

Ballet and Butterflies

"So we are always confident, even though we know that
as long as we live in these bodies we are not at home in
the Lord. For we live by believing and not by seeing."
2 Corinthians 5:6–7 (New Living Translation)

On the campus of Stanford University in good old California, nestled between Campus Drive and the Oval is one of the focal points of knowledge concerning mitochondrial diseases. Specifically, the Lucile Packard Children's Hospital, part of Stanford Medicine, is one of the top care centers for Mito. A couple of mental footnotes here: First, I use the plural *mitochondrial diseases* because there are many types. Second, for argument's sake, there are several other "focal points of knowledge," such as Tufts Medical Center in Boston, Massachusetts, Columbia University in New York, and notable locations in Australia, such as Melbourne and Brisbane, among others.

From the United Mitochondrial Disease Foundation (UMDF) website, www.umdf.org: "Mitochondrial diseases are a group of progressive metabolic, often neurological disorders, which result from defects in the mitochondria, which are in almost every type of cell in the body. Mitochondria are responsible for creating more than 90% of the energy needed to sustain life and support growth. Mitochondrial failure results in energy deprivation within the cells. Cell injury and even cell death follow. If this process repeats throughout the body, whole systems begin to fail and the affected person's life becomes severely compromised. The disease primarily affects children, but adult onset is becoming increasingly common. Diseases of the mitochondria appear to cause the most damage to organs requiring high energy levels including: brain, heart, liver, skeletal muscles, kidney, eyes, and the endocrine and respiratory systems."

Anatomy of a Cell

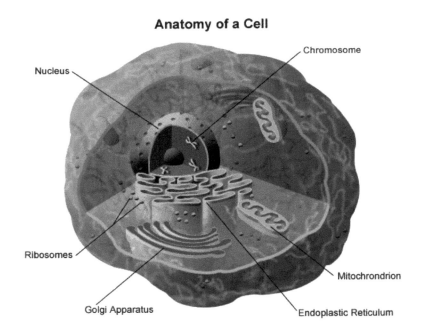

(Drawing courtesy of www.ianlogan.co.uk)

Microscopic photo of a single mitochondria inside a cardiac muscle cell

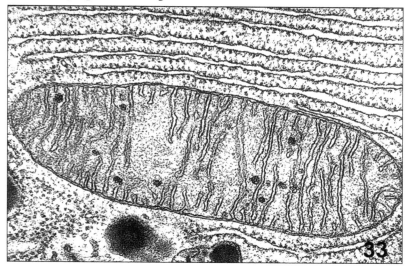

(Photo courtesy of www.histologyatlas.wisc.edu.)

With names like mitochondrial encephalomyopathy, Kearns-Sayre syndrome, and myoclonus epilepsy with ragged red fibers (MERRF), you can see why I will leave the majority of further research to you to do on your own. But from the above list of bodily systems, it's easy to see how and why Mito is a serious threat to a healthy human body. More than one in four thousand children born each year in the United States will develop a mitochondrial disease by age ten.[1] Most cases are inherited, with males and females equally affected. Additionally, "the World Health Organization (WHO) calculated that neurodegenerative diseases, also associated with mitochondrial dysfunction, will become the world's second leading cause of death by the year 2040. There are very few effective treatments and no cure."[2]

Annually, there are quite a few events, support groups, information nights, walkathons, and symposiums hosted by the Australian Mitochondrial Disease Foundation (AMDF) and the UMDF, yet there is a great need for funding. The Caulfield campus of Monash University in Caulfield, Australia, was host to AussieMit 2012, the southern hemisphere's premiere mitochondrial science conference. According to the AMDF website, approximately one hundred eighty scientists and doctors attended, most from Australasia, but many from centers of mitochondrial excellence in other parts of the world. This biennial event occurred in Perth, Australia, in 2014 and in Sydney in 2016. In 2018, the event took place in Melbourne and had at least one speaker from the United States: Jared Rutter, PhD, a biochemistry professor from the University of Utah.

The important event brings together scientists and clinicians studying biochemistry, molecular biology, plant sciences, and cell and developmental biology with mitochondria as the focal point. On the UMDF site, one can find many resources, event info, and clinical patient registries that are a tremendous asset to affected families and to Mito research efforts.

One of the favorite Mito events worldwide has been "World Stay in Bed Day," which, as you might guess, brings attention to the fact that many Mito sufferers are bedridden and cannot function as the majority of us do physically. During this event, a bunch of people from across the globe stay in bed in their pajamas all day. Sounds like an event my kids would have really liked. If you want a quick and excellent explanation of what Mito is, read the short but information-packed eleven-page book by Martine Vanderspuy called, *A Little Book about MiTO*.[3] Even better, read it with your youngster.

Meanwhile, back to my friend and the reason I'm telling this story—Bonnie Belle. On October 4, 1983, a bouncing baby girl named Bonnie Marie Codier was born in Phoenix, Arizona, to Lyn and Dave Codier. There were no obvious medical issues at the moment of birth, except that Bonnie's mom, Lyn, had to wait at least two hours to see and hold Bonnie (even with good APGAR scores),[4] without any explanation from doctors and nurses as to why.

Bonnie showed early that she possessed, at least what she considered to be, normal levels of energy in everyday activities overall, but specifically on the ballet floor. She became tired sometimes and had to rest often, but as Bonnie explained, "I simply thought that was normal."

Bonnie began dance, ballet, tap, and gymnastics at five years old and remembered starting to have heart "flip-flops," as she called them, and fast heart rates that began at about nine years old. She just didn't tell anyone until she was about twelve.

Those of you who appreciate the beauty and athleticism of ballet, have you ever heard of a gentleman named David Hallberg? Mr. Hallberg is an American classical ballet dancer, a principal dancer with the American Ballet Theater, resident guest artist with the Australian Ballet, and formerly a principal dancer with the world-famous Russian Bolshoi Ballet, beginning in 2011.[5] He is the first ever American-born principal dancer for the Bolshoi. He was born in Rapid City, South Dakota, and grew up in Phoenix, Arizona. He trained at the School of Ballet Arizona, along with a certain friend of mine: Bonnie. They remained friends for years, and Mr. Hallberg sent a signed copy of one of his Bolshoi programs in late 2013 to Bonnie, along with a personal note of good wishes inside. Reading his note to Bonnie, it was clear he had a lot of respect for her, both as a person and as a ballet talent with whom he had practiced. Bonnie told me she had a tremendous respect for David as well and really appreciated the program he sent. Even more so, she appreciated the personal note inside.

Imagine the craft, sport, or other hobby or talent that you consider your best. Imagine being so good at it that you had gone as far as you could go locally and were planning to attend the top school in New York, with the thought that you would make that craft your profession, working alongside the likes of the best-in-the-business talent. Then, one day, you find yourself on the floor, unable to move after one of your practices. An hour later, you find yourself in a hospital, with multiple medical staff having no idea what ails you. All you know is that you won't be able to pursue your dream any longer. Bonnie found herself in this situation in the beginning of 1995 at age twelve.

Over the next eight years, her entire teen years, Bonnie spent more time being transported by her loving, nurse-trained parents and emergency vehicles to hospitals and intensive care units in multiple states than most of us will in our lifetimes. It's no wonder Bonnie began to love the butterfly, often thought of as a symbol of freedom, something she surely at times felt robbed of, as most of us would have in her situation. Whenever I saw Bonnie, it was always very probable that at least one shimmering butterfly would be fluttering somewhere near her. Every time my wife and I see one today, we think and talk of her.

Bonnie spent long periods of time in the hospital—once for four months, another time for seven months, and even a year at a time. Bonnie was admitted to the hospital at least thirty-three times in the eleven-year period from age fourteen until she was twenty-four. Due to their limited knowledge of Mito, her doctors not only didn't understand what was ailing her, they even at times questioned whether Bonnie was being mistreated by her parents and hinted that maybe Bonnie herself was sneaking drugs or other medication, causing her medical issues.

She traveled from Abrazo Arizona Heart Hospital to Scottsdale Healthcare, Good Samaritan Medical Center to Desert Samaritan Medical Center, Mayo Clinic Scottsdale to Mayo Clinic Rochester,

Massachusetts General Hospital to Maine Medical Center, and Desert Samaritan back to Good Samaritan. The first mention of mitochondrial disease as a possible cause of Bonnie's symptoms was in February 2004 when Bonnie was twenty years old. It wasn't until 2006, two years later, that doctors made a definitive diagnosis. Ten years of Bonnie's life had passed, with her feeling a lot like a medical experiment.

I don't mean for this partial list of health care providers and the evaluations and services they provided Bonnie over the years as an indictment of any of them. As a matter of fact, I have about twenty years of varied health care experience, am employed by Banner Health myself (formerly with Scottsdale Healthcare, now Honor Health), and believe these are excellent health care systems. This discussion is meant to show the dire need for further knowledge and research in the area of mitochondrial disease, so that children born with similar unexplained symptoms today will experience some degree less pain, discomfort, surgeries, medical cost, and personal and family stress that comes from knowing that there remains no cure today for a loved one with Mito.

Imagine also the lack of personal dignity that comes with being bedridden each and every day, even as family and other well-wishers visit. We often take for granted the basic freedoms that any person confined to a bed is lacking.

I remember visiting Bonnie one Christmas—her favorite time of the year, celebrating the twelve days of Christmas and the birth of Jesus. There were her family members and a couple of close friends, all sitting in a circle, sharing a laugh in the large Arizona room of their home, with Bonnie lying in bed, smack in the middle of them. Bonnie didn't *try* to be the center of attention. She simply *was*. Bonnie had compassion for homebound people of all ages that were limited in joining in the festivities. She was especially interested in this group of people who didn't have a way to get to church and experience the in-person relationships, greetings, handshakes, and hugs that public worship offers.

Bonnie and her older brother, Sean, were homeschooled by their mom, Lyn, who had nurse training and who was developing her own music school, later to be known, and thrive, as Lyn's Musikgarten. Bonnie's brother, Sean, went on to become a physician. Bonnie's dad, Dave, was a trained nurse who moved up the ranks through the years to hospital environmental services and security director positions in Arizona at Banner Health. Bonnie benefited from a trained nurse father and an astute nurse mother who, for many years, provided together twenty-four seven care that equated to four full-time nurses per day.

Bonnie had several pets over the years, but her favorite was her playful six-pound Yorkie named Mallie. Mallie moved so quickly around their home that they had to leave a four-foot leash connected to her body at all times or they'd never catch her. Mallie joined the family in all their cross-country van trips to Boston or Stanford University. She became one of the most traveled, cultured little canines you could ever meet!

Bonnie celebrated many birthdays and holidays in the hospital. She had a pacemaker and a double vascular port, a device that allows someone who needs long-term IV therapy to receive medicine, liquid food, blood, or treatments for a long period of time. These ports allow someone to receive efficient treatments at home, at a clinic, or in a hospital. Bonnie required daily IV medications and fluid, as well as oxygen therapy and lab blood draws several times each week. She had her gall bladder, spleen, thymus, and colon removed. Mito affected every organ system in her body and caused adrenal failure, fatty acid deficiency, and polycystic ovarian disease, as well as kidney issues and other problems. Because of her severely impaired immunity, she required IVIG therapy every three weeks, which provided an intravenous infusion of needed antibodies to help her fight infections that can become life-threatening. Bonnie was unable to walk due to profound muscle weakness and was bed-bound, but she used an electric wheelchair when she needed to be transported. She also had chronic gastrointestinal bleeding, thus requiring blood transfusions every three to five weeks. Bonnie and her family were very appreciative of blood donors, as these gifts added years to her life.

Bonnie had a complicated and severe form of this disease. Experts have stated that hers is one of the most complicated cases they have seen. And while research is showing that in *other* diseases it is more and more common to find a mitochondrial *component* involved, it's still rare to have Bonnie's presentation of this disease. In cases like hers, it's a terminal condition, although the timing of the worsening progression is unknown. Bonnie, in her own words, had firm faith that God would sustain her, regardless of the disease, until she had finished the work He had for her on Earth. Further, she believed that if her work finished tomorrow, no amount of human intervention would be able to prevent Him from taking her home.

What *was* Bonnie's work, you ask? She served so that as many people as possible would know God's love and Word because of her life. Bonnie continued her fight with multiple medical problems, but lived her life joyfully to its fullest, all to God's glory. Bonnie's dream was to see a Mito research facility be developed that could help keep children from going through the same struggles she went through by increasing knowledge of the disease and helping to find a treatment.

For me to experience firsthand the discomfort and challenges that Bonnie experienced every single day, while simultaneously seeing and feeling the joy that she shared with others, formed a comparison that I was quite sure I shouldn't make in relation to my own attitudes. Unfortunately, for me, I just couldn't help it. I just kept thinking what Bonnie could do with a healthy body—one like mine.

Bonnie's Journal Entry #2, August 27

Hello, Family and Friends,

We are back home from a trip to the East Coast to see my mito doc and get out of the heat. We had a nice time seeing some of the family (since none of them live near us in AZ), and realized more clearly than ever how much the extreme heat takes out of me.

Just before we left to travel East, I called to inquire about the results of a skin biopsy I had taken prior to leaving Phoenix. I got a call while back East from the medical assistant, apologizing profusely, because my biopsy had been LOST! Well, no wonder I didn't get a phone call (prior to leaving)! Isn't that such a crazy thing? And, even crazier, is that this is not the first, or the second, or even the third or fourth time this kind of thing has happened. I won't go into detail, but I have had so many incidents with biopsies, cultures, labs, etc., getting messed up or lost. I definitely have the "Murphy's Law" life. I really have to believe in God's sovereignty when these things happen, because they are inexplicable, and I would otherwise go insane always being the "one" that these things happen to.

Well, as usual, thank you so much to the people who pray for me. It is truly those prayers and the hand of God that keep me going. In addition to all the current crazy health stuff, there have been other areas that have caused stress, frustration, depression, etc., and it's been hard having that load continue to be ongoing. I won't go into detail now, but just know that there are "other" things, on top of the health stuff. Back East I got to see a special friend for only the 2ⁿᵈ or 3ʳᵈ time in my life (but someone who stays updated on me and prays), and when he walked in, the first thing he said was, "How is the battle?" He understands that my life is a battle, a hard fought one, one that doesn't get any easier, it just gets harder as fatigue and lack of resolution continue with each day that goes by. There are no breaks from this fight, even for people who endure trials. It is usually for different seasons, with some "breaks" in between the storms, but my life is a constant downpour. The fact that I have not succumbed to the battle is huge evidence of God's sustaining grace and of His strength in me to keep fighting it.

Speaking of storms, we are currently in the middle of a monsoon thunderstorm, so I should probably finish this up (it has been quite long already!). God's blessings be upon you!

Love and Hugs,

Bonnie ☺

3

OKIE FROM MUSKOGEE

"Train up a child in the way he should go; and when he is old, he will not depart from it." **Proverbs 22:6** (King James Version)

I was born on June 7, 1959, in Norman, Oklahoma, to Charles and Doris Sanders. All my memories and recollections of both my parents and all my siblings are wonderful. There was never a time when I did not know one hundred percent that my parents loved me. I have one first-class older brother named Phil and three of the most wonderful younger sisters you could ever find: Margaret, Nora, and Amy. My first memories were of rural Muskogee, Oklahoma, prior to kindergarten, sitting on the sofa watching the snow and ice storms take turns powdering and crystallizing our living room window, while my brother, Phil, read Dr. Seuss books to me.

Another of those early memories in Muskogee was playing outside in the grass with my siblings in the summer afternoon and as late into the evening as we could until our parents called us in for dinner. One of those evenings, we all came running in to slide around the booth bench of our diner-style round table, only to notice that my sister, Margaret, had a large round gray tick attached to the middle of her forehead, totally unknown to her. As she sat there, smiling in childlike ignorance of the situation wondering why everyone was staring at her, my dad tried to explain to her that she shouldn't worry. He was going to calmly and professionally hold a lit match near the tick on her forehead until it felt the heat and voluntarily removed its hold on her skin. Between the other kids' laughter mixed with some amount of horror, we all watched as Margaret held her head remarkably still and trusted Dad to remove the creature without harming her in the least. I'm thinking about writing a novel about this situation someday and plan to call it *Tick Talk*. Watch for it.

Operation successful, we moved on to helping ourselves to whatever was on the table—probably something like masa harina tortillas with a vegetable, beans, and macaroni and cheese—and for dessert, "candy," which was my dad's name for butter and honey mixed together with a spoon and spread on a piece of bread. Yes, that is what we call "Oklahoma Gourmet."

As the years passed and I grew to little league baseball age, the positive aspects of having an older brother became clear relatively quickly. To be able to simply grab our baseball gloves and ball at any time of the day and go tearing out the door to the lot next door to play catch and practice together was amazing. Not only that, Phil liked the catcher position, while I—you guessed it—became a pitcher. How better to get to know each other's tendencies than to practice together every day. I have Phil to thank for a few little league no-hitters and winning the local Pitch, Hit, and Throw competition at a young age. Now it's referred to as Pitch, Hit, and Run. Somewhere down the line, someone must have said, "Hey, pitching and throwing are somewhat similar. Maybe we should rename that!"

Phil was and still is a very good athlete on his own, and he was my own personal trainer before they were cool. By the way, Phil didn't know he was my personal trainer, so don't tell him I said that. I have to put it that way, because he's one-upped me on so many occasions. One example was his earning his Centurion patch for his part in navigating and helping land his Navy EA-6B aircraft *one hundred times* on aircraft carriers. By the time he retired, he had over three hundred landings, or traps, as they call them. I asked him a few years back to tell me the scariest situation he had ever been in during those Navy days. He responded, "Trying to trap the plane on the USS Nimitz off the coast of Alaska, while the carrier was careening up and down on waves high enough to splash over the sixty foot-high deck of the carrier."

As I remember, I didn't have much to say to that one.

Our other favorite pastime in those days of growing up was for Phil and I to put on our heaviest coats and tie up, padded hoods (we were fortunate enough to have warm coats) and go outside with our football to play a one-on-one tackle game in the side yard. We'd rake together as many leaves as we could to make a soft landing area, then line up and run right at each other for an hour or two. It was incredible fun. We would do it now, but I live in Arizona and Phil lives in Florida, so we don't have thick-enough coats for padding.

In junior high, my dad showed up one day with a tennis ball and a couple of old, wooden tennis racquets that he had rustled up somewhere. I'm still wondering where he got that tennis ball. He took Phil and me out to the local tennis court in Hobart, Oklahoma, to expose us to the game. We both immediately loved it, even with only one dead ball to learn with and those pesky blades of grass growing out of the cracks in the court. We spent more time chasing balls than hitting them, but we were both hooked. We excelled in tennis in high school and our freshman years of college and have been very active in senior tennis leagues and tournaments as we've grown older.

Memory after memory of sports, smiles, and siblings filled my days growing up in Oklahoma and a short stint in Telluride, Colorado, during first grade. Sometimes we didn't have that much to eat, but we really didn't know it. My mom and dad always made sure that we ate first, and they took what was left.

One Sunday morning during church in Lone Wolf, Oklahoma, our Baptist pastor introduced a recent ex-convict named Butch to the crowd, asking if anyone might allow him to stay at their home for a few weeks. Butch had just been released from a nearby prison. My mother, Doris, raised her hand immediately and said that we would be happy to do so. Looking around at my siblings's faces, I was not sure that *we* represented my entire family of seven, but hey. What can you do? Butch was about six foot, four inches tall and weighed around two hundred and thirty pounds (according to my honest recollection), including his well-manicured crew cut. He squeezed in and rode home in the car with us that day after church. We had lunch, and, after, he ended up staying with the seven of us for almost the entire planned three weeks. This was just long enough for him to physically rough me up a few times, hold me under water at the local pool for what seemed like a couple of minutes, then finally steal our car and leave town. The police found the car burned like a crisp marshmallow in Texas somewhere. So much for sharing God's mercy and grace with others, I thought. If I'd have been old enough, I think I might have asked my mom, "How did that work out for ya?"

Funny thing is, my mom continued to treat people like that. She's now eighty-seven and going strong.

As our siblings got a little older, my middle sister, Nora, began suffering from painful migraine headaches and seizures. Four of us ended up suffering from migraines over time, even though our brilliant family doctor told my mom to her face that it was impossible for four of her children to have migraines. I remember Nora was once sitting in a living room chair having an apparent seizure. I was big enough to help and quickly scooped her up in my arms to transfer her quickly to her bed. Meanwhile, she, even more quickly, vomited down the front of my clothes. I've reminded her about that for years. That event didn't seem to bother her much—then or now.

My brother and I also came up with a strange mix of adventure and exercise. Utilizing the unharvested wheat field next to our house near Lone Wolf, Oklahoma, we would sneak out into the field when we noticed one of the beautiful gray and black Gleaner G combines moving into the field to cut the wheat several hundred yards away. Still pretty small, we would hunker down in the tall, waving wheat and hide until the combine got near us, gauging our time of escape until the thrump-thrump-thrump noise of the combine's blades got too near for comfort. Then we would run screaming to pick another spot to hide in and wait again, laughing. We made the mistake of telling our mom about this when we were in our thirties. We should have waited a couple more decades.

One thing that my brother and I are especially thankful for is that my dad taught us to paint houses at an early age. I was about eight years old and Phil was about ten. We weren't appreciative at the time of getting up every Saturday morning around 6:00 a.m. in the dark to have a quick breakfast and hop in the truck to drive to work. We are thankful now, though, for Dad teaching us to work, to work hard, and to learn a trade. We can paint our own houses or most anything else we need to paint and do it professionally. I received a list from a close friend several years back of twenty things a man should know how to do and being able to paint his house was one of them. You won't get any argument from me there. My brother and I have some quite funny stories that I could share about those painting days with Dad, but I'll save that for another time. We both used those painting talents through high school and college to help ourselves financially.

Throughout high school in Norman, Oklahoma, my siblings and I were all sports-minded and blessed with good health, unlike Bonnie. Even though our family didn't have much money, God always seemed to provide us with what we needed. I was lucky to be able to drive an old, faded red 1962 Volkswagen Beetle when I received my driver's license. At least I drove it until I forgot to put oil in it for several weeks and it caught on fire on the I-35 freeway near town. It took me a few moments to recognize the hand signal for *YOUR CAR IS ON FIRE!!!* from a distressed motorist in the next lane.

I often read books while growing up. Our family didn't have a television full-time until I was a junior in high school. Looking back, I wouldn't trade that time without a television for anything. I remember renting a TV to watch the Montreal Summer Olympics in 1976. Prior to that, if I wasn't playing baseball, football, basketball, or tennis, I was reading a book. It didn't hurt that my dad worked in sales for Random House publishers for a while. There were a few extra books around the house during that time.

Dad was a school teacher for years until he decided to grow a mustache over the 1970 summer break in Lone Wolf, Oklahoma. As the fall school session was getting ready to begin, the cigar-smoking school superintendent asked my dad to shave his mustache prior to the first day of school. My dad first replied, "Sure, no problem." Then, after thinking about it for a few hours, he decided not to shave it. The school district fired him for showing up with it still intact on the first day of school, and it became a pretty big story in the area. He ended up suing the school district and winning the court case three years later, but, of course, the attorneys ended up with any money that could have helped our family. At least my dad didn't ruin any high school boys' lives by being a bad example and wearing a mustache in front of them! The horrors. After that, he began working at Random House.

My parents divorced when I was a senior in high school. Although somewhat surprising, I wouldn't call it traumatic for my brother or me. I worried more about how it might affect my three younger sisters, though they all seemed to come out of it just fine.

By the time I was a senior in high school, I was fairly set in my worldview and my Biblical Christian beliefs. I knew my mom and dad loved my siblings and me unconditionally, no matter what differences they had. The interesting part was the dichotomy of my parent's beliefs and my thoughts about what they believed while they were raising us.

Since our family went together to Baptist church most Sunday mornings, evenings, and Wednesday nights, as well as to local revivals growing up, I assumed that my mom and dad were united in their worldview and spiritual beliefs. I remember driving from western Oklahoma to Oklahoma City in junior high for my parents to speak to some folks about possibly working as missionaries. We never became a missionary family and this plan wasn't spoken about with us kids much, if at all, but I picked up on where we were going that day.

It wasn't until my senior year in high school, as my dad and I were leaving a track meet in Oklahoma City at the Myriad Center and returning to Norman, that my dad said as I drove home, "Yeah. When you mature, you will realize that all that belief in a supernatural god is a bunch of bull."

I remember cruising along at sixty-five miles per hour and looking over at him in the passenger seat wondering which field, right or left, that came from. We didn't discuss it much on that drive. Later, I respectfully said to him, "Dad, just because you have decided to go off on another path, don't expect us kids to follow you."

I very much respect and love my dad, although we have very different worldviews. I couldn't have asked for a better father growing up. He taught me about science, to work hard, to never stop learning, and to love your neighbor as yourself, no matter what their background, color, or belief. But he has continued to grow more atheistic (he prefers nontheistic) in his beliefs over the years, while my mom is as strong a believer in Biblical Christianity as anyone I know. It brings out some interesting conversations.

Getting married at twenty-six years old in 1985 felt quite normal. I felt one hundred percent that I was with the right person and was excited to begin this new stage of my life. My wife and I had been married for five years and just moved from Oklahoma to Arizona when we decided to grow our family. We were living in an apartment in Scottsdale, Arizona, and I was working thirty-two hours a week at a local hospital while also finishing my business degree at Arizona State University full-time when we had our first child, Bradley, in 1990. Our second child, my one and only favorite daughter, Korey, followed in 1991 and then our third, another wonderful son, Tommy, in 1994.

After buying a new home and being married for seventeen years, my wife and I divorced in 2002. This is just a small snippet of my imperfect life, so far. I learned there is enough blame to go around for all of our human imperfections.

During those many trips to church as a youngster, I had heard and memorized Romans 3:23 (King James Version), which reads, "For all have sinned, and come short of the glory of God." Sometimes this verse bothers people who don't realize that they might just be a sinner. It didn't take me long to realize that most humans don't like to think of themselves as sinners. Looking back, this verse never bothered me. If you can get through the book of Romans and still stay engaged, you may be on the right track. Or, you may simply have thicker skin than most of us.

As I mentioned, my life is not perfect. There was the divorce from my children's mother, who is a great mom and wonderful lady, by the way. My second marriage a couple of years later ended in my second wife leaving me for her own reasons. I wouldn't be showing God's grace if I elaborated, so I won't. Then, a personal bankruptcy followed my second marriage, and financial struggles ensued. Following that, I dealt with people telling my children negative things about me. Again, I had the choice to be angry and respond negatively or forgive and lay this worldly imperfection at the feet of the Lord.

Along with the help of some friends from my church, especially Jim Harper, my good friend and our community pastor at the time, I was able to work through most feelings of anger or betrayal and move those feelings toward forgiveness. Please note I said *most* feelings of anger or betrayal. Being in the Word and sharing the Word with several groups of guys from East Valley Bible Church (now Redemption Church), helped tremendously. It's amazing how we can sometimes feel like we are the only one in the world going through what we are going through, only to find out as we engage with other folks in our communities that many people are having similar struggles. During this period of dealing with the most difficult times I've had so far in my life, I found that the more time I spent in quiet time with the Lord, the better and easier things became. Surprise, surprise.

In 2008, on the suggestion of some close friends from East Valley Bible Church, Gwen and David Lucas, I made a call for a date with a girl named Kimberly. Gwen and Dave had known Kimberly for ten years and thought we should meet. I asked Kimberly to play nine holes of golf for our first date, and she accepted. We had a great time and both felt by the second date, a dinner with the Lucas family, that this was a special relationship. I found out some interesting things about Kimberly. First, she divorced her first husband and, looking back, realized that it was wrong to do so. Second, she remarried and then lost her second husband to mental illness and suicide. When one admittedly imperfect person meets another admittedly imperfect person, and both realize that it is only by God's grace, brought to them by the substitutionary atonement of Jesus Christ's death on the cross and His resurrection, there is a gift of freedom that they'll receive nowhere else on this earth. Kimberly and I quickly agreed "And we know that God causes everything to work together for the good of those who love God and are called according to His purpose for them," as stated in Romans 8:28 (New Living Translation). There's that pesky book of Romans again.

Kimberly and I were married in October 2009 and both agree there is nothing more important to us than spending the remainder of our lives doing something that glorifies our Sovereign God, His son Jesus Christ, and the Holy Spirit within us. We realize that we will not reach perfection in this endeavor while we are on this earth.

After meeting Bonnie, I noticed the number of people that she positively affected with her constant attitude of gratitude, whether in person, by phone or email, or from her blog, CaringBridge, which reached over three hundred fifty thousand visitors at my last check. Of course, I compared the results of Bonnie bringing light to people of all ages, despite confinement to a bed, with my own results as a physically healthy and active person. I realized quickly that this comparison was not going to make me look very good! Oh, well. The intrigue alone was worth the time spent thinking about it.

So I asked myself, Why haven't I made as positive of an impact on other people's lives as Bonnie has with her limitations, yet I have the physical blessings God has given me?

I began thinking more and more about what type of light, if any, I'd personally been to the world so far. Bonnie had proven to me that one does not need a healthy body to be a lighthouse to the world. Have you ever heard of Joni Eareckson Tada? She is a Christian author of over fifty books, a singer, a talk show host, and founder and CEO of the Joni and Friends International Disability Center, among other things, who suffered a diving accident in 1967 at seventeen years old, becoming a quadriplegic. If you've not heard of Joni, haven't read her autobiography, *Joni*, or seen the feature film of the same name, please look her up. You will literally *feel* her light and joy in finding God's grace in the midst of daily challenges. In fact, one of Bonnie's favorite quotes in the entire world comes from Joni: "God points to the peaceful attitude of suffering people to teach others about Himself."

Bonnie would often use a piece of her finest stationery to handwrite one of her favorite quotes, imprint her butterfly stamp on it, then give it to someone or post it in her room. And this quote is one that Bonnie gave to me (see photo). This special card has a permanent place on my writing desk.

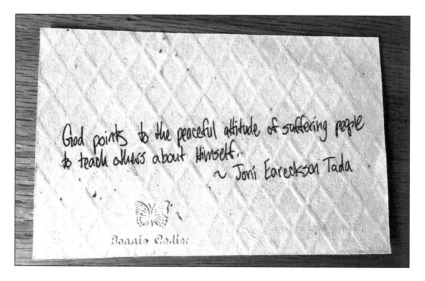

I asked myself, What is it that a person needs to serve others? What is the code that should drive me? The first answer that came to me was compassion—a true caring for my neighbors. All of them.

Bonnie's Journal Entry #3, December 7

(Sent from Lyn, Bonnie's mummy):

Just a quick update on Bonnie—she is fighting a staph bacteremia; gut has shut down and she is in a lot of pain.

More spiking fevers and rigors … thought we would be done with that. Antibiotics were started early last evening. Thank you for your prayers, Bonnie is doing her best to fight this. She is in a lot of pain.

4

Compassion Works

"Finally, all of you should be of one mind. Sympathize with each other. Love each other as brothers and sisters. Be tender-hearted and keep a humble attitude." **1 Peter 3:8** (New Living Translation)

Compassion. Have you ever looked that word up in the dictionary? Depending upon which dictionary you look in, you will get something like "compassion (kəm-ˈpa-shən): sorrow for the sufferings or troubles of another; with the urge to help; pity; deep sympathy."

The dictionary that I looked it up in, *Webster's New World Dictionary*, was copyrighted in 1961. This thick dictionary, with a binding that is falling apart, is one thousand, one hundred eighty-one pages, and includes an encyclopedic section, which is very informative and has been neatly stacked in my family bookshelves since I can remember. When its pages are opened, the smell is one that I distinctly remember from when I was about eight years old. I just now randomly opened to and smelled page six hundred eighty-five to remind myself. I'm not sure how I ended up with this book since it has my brother's name written in the front of it in my mom's handwriting, and I have four siblings. I'm pretty sure if my dad knew I had it, he would soon be on his way to get it. Oh, well. The cat is out of the bag now, so to speak.

If you are thinking that in 1961 there weren't enough known English language words to fill one thousand, one hundred eighty-one pages at normal print size, you may be onto something. This dictionary also included some extra items, as I mentioned: an encyclopedic section; weights and measures; a guide to English grammar; a dictionary of musical terms; a dictionary of medical terms; a business manual; a section on Parliamentary Law; a list of the presidents of the United States through John F. Kennedy; the U.S. Declaration of Independence; and, of course, some household information and more, believe it or not. Lest you think that this household information would not be useful, check this info out: *"Eggs—keep in covered container in the refrigerator. Storing eggs with large end up helps to keep the yolk centered."*[6]

Are *your* yolks centered?

The above wealth of information would normally be enough, but something in the foreword of the dictionary caught my eye—the following line, which was only one of several that, according to the publication, attempts to bring the greatest possible usefulness to any reader of the dictionary: *"Those obsolete and archaic terms and senses that are frequently found in the Bible or in other standard works of literature have been included."*[7]

What? I mean, wow. Forget "obsolete and archaic," at least for the moment. After all the amazing bits of information I've learned over the last half century, I think I just read that the Bible was just another "standard work of literature." That sounds like a subject for another book and seems to contradict the words of Noah Webster, himself.

Founding father and educator Noah Webster (1758–1843) said:

> "The moral principles and precepts contained in the scriptures ought to form the basis of all our civil constitutions and laws. All the miseries and evils which men suffer from vice, crime, ambition, injustice, oppression, slavery, and war, proceed from their despising or neglecting the precepts contained in the Bible."[8]

I like this guy.

Maybe I simply interpreted that sentence in the dictionary incorrectly. Since portions of the U.S. Constitution, the Declaration of Independence, the Mayflower Compact, State Constitutions, and other American founding documents have many references, concepts, and quotations from the Holy Bible, I would put the Bible in a class *above* "standard works of literature." Additionally, since the Holy Bible is God's Word, anyone who believes the Bible is God's Word would, no doubt, deem it more important than a "standard work of literature."

By the way, speaking of "works of literature" and the idea of compassion working, *does* compassion work?

Do we simply feel that compassion helps? Or when we say compassion works, does our mind tend to move to the subject of doing good works?

Are they works of compassion or other works that we humans hope will earn some standing for us somewhere?

Speaking of a subject for another book, the discussion of whether the good deeds that many people do are simply a result of God's love shining through them, or that good works are required good deeds that we must constantly remember to perform in order to earn our way to a better place, would be an interesting topic. Interesting especially for people who feel compelled to show compassion for others, in one or more of many ways.

It can actually be confusing to hear someone tell you that the Bible contradicts itself in this area, with the Apostle Paul in Romans 4:5 (New Living Translation) telling listeners, "But people are counted as righteous, not because of their work, but because of their faith in God who forgives sinners."[9]

Not long after, however, we hear that a man named James, who was the brother of Jesus and wrote the Biblical book of James, states in James 2:26 (New Living Translation), "Just as the body is dead without breath, so also faith is dead without good works."

Hmm. Are works important? Or not important?

I'm obviously not a theologian, but I'm sure that with some further investigation into the context, one can comfortably conclude that the teachings of Paul and James are not at odds. As the Life Application Study Bible so clearly states, "While it is true that our good deeds can never *earn salvation*, true faith always results in a changed life and good deeds."[10]

Or, as my mom recently reminded me during a visit out to Arizona, "The love of Christ constrains us to do good works."

We don't have to listen to our mothers after we turn 50, do we?

Back to centering my yolks.

I never thought much about compassion or works growing up, whatever they meant, as both my mother and father were always nice and helpful to everyone. (Remember our friend, Butch, from church?) Remember my dad trying to assist someone by siphoning gas from his truck to theirs and ending up with leaded fuel in his mouth? Oh, I didn't share that one with you. Never mind. Since my parents showed compassion as a rule, I didn't have much for comparison. So, when I first answered that email request in 2011 from Abe and Joy De la Rosa in the Compassion Ministries of Redemption Church, Gilbert, Arizona, about helping a family, I thought it sounded like a good way to show my good side. In other words, I was sure in my heart I could be a blessing to the Codier family.

The request was to simply go by the Codier home on a Sunday after-noon, say around 4:30 p.m., and be there with Bonnie while her parents, Dave and Lyn, went to church from about 5:00 p.m. to 6:30 p.m. They would be back around 6:45 p.m., and I would drive back home, about a fifteen minute drive. They called it Bonnie-sitting. The plan was that I would try it once, see how it went (see if Bonnie could put up with me), and then possibly be a blessing once every month or two, depending on how many other folks helped out through Compassion Ministries. My wife worked almost every Sunday afternoon doing new home sales, so I thought, Hey. What would it hurt? For years, I had thought about showing my compas-sion for others, but something often got in the way. Imagine that.

There was some excitement surrounding that first visit to Bonnie-sit in April of 2011. The description itself, Bonnie-sit, that I first heard from Bonnie's mom, Lyn, gave credence to the fact that I was going to apparently be spending time with someone who greatly needed me. I liked that, as I have somewhat of a serving spirit, which reminds me of my mom and my dad. Upon my arrival at the Codier's front door, Mallie, that little six-pound turbo ball of dog hair wearing a leash that trolled the floor behind her, greeted me first. We became friends quite quickly as I sat down to five or ten minutes with Bonnie's parents and watched Mallie run circles around the coffee table. After that general introduction, Dave and Lyn took me in to meet Bonnie in her bedroom, which could better be described as a den in the center of their home with a door entering from the hallway, double French doors to the kitchen, and a window looking out to the rear yard and the nearby urban waterway. The use of that room for Bonnie's bedroom made it easier to transport Bonnie in and out, as well as being more central for all the life-supporting connections that were involved.

I didn't have many expectations meeting Bonnie or her parents. Bonnie Belle, as her close friends knew her, had recently turned twenty-eight years old and was an attractive young lady with a beautiful smile and warm eyes. She was lying in her bed, comfortably dressed with several pillows propping her head up, and was connected to an oxygen supply. We shook hands and I took a seat in the chair about six feet away from her bed. The four of us chatted for three or four more minutes and then Dave and Lyn headed off to church. I was a little surprised that I wasn't told about some super-secret safety precautions, maybe a red phone or something. After all, I knew that Bonnie was terminally ill with no known cure. What if something happened in the middle of Dave and Lyn singing "Amazing Grace?"

I received my answer after only spending a short time getting to know Bonnie. Besides being an incredibly sharp young lady because of her homeschooling, she literally whitewashed me with her smiles, obvious joy, and appreciation for life.

Note I said joy, not happiness. You can't physically be happy about living without personal dignity, as I mentioned earlier. Bonnie couldn't simply interrupt one of my stories with "Hold that thought," jump up, and pop into the bathroom for thirty seconds, then return to hear the rest of the story. Same with other visitors during a normal week or holiday visitors filling up the room while she rested in the middle of it. Most of us take for granted the types of issues that concern personal dignity and hygiene.

I mentioned earlier some of the life-sustaining systems that Bonnie was connected to and some of the surgeries she had. I also mentioned that Bonnie often spent her birthdays or other holidays in the hospital. Try handling that stress while being questioned about possibly using unauthorized prescriptions found in the home. Going through the pain, discomfort, and questions of why that Bonnie has gone through for years, coupled with physicians who don't understand mitochondrial disease and accuse her parents of possibly mistreating her, would remove some happiness, wouldn't it? It became quickly obvious to me that Bonnie had a true joy—one that came from her sovereign God, Jesus Christ, and the Holy Spirit.

I remember leaving Bonnie's home that night feeling very different than I thought I would. That is one expectation that, being honest, I did have. I assumed that I would leave her home feeling somewhat proud of being there for her, assisting her, and giving her parents the opportunity to leave the house and go to church, knowing Bonnie was taken care of. Nothing could be further from the truth. I, instead, left *knowing*, not just feeling, that Bonnie had done the blessing! Near the end of my visit that night, Bonnie grabbed a small notepad and a pen and scribbled something on it. She carefully tore out the piece of paper, leaned forward, and handed it to me. It read, "Always be joyful. Never stop praying. Be thankful in all circumstances." She'd written a series of letters and numbers below her beautiful handwriting: 1T51618.

I thought, Oh, boy. Here we go. A puzzle from the smart, homeschooled girl. Just wait, smarty-pants, until I get my iPhone out. I'll have this one figured out in no time.

As the front door opened a few minutes later and Bonnie's parents walked in the front door, I folded and stuffed the piece of paper in my jeans pocket, thanked Bonnie for a wonderful couple of hours getting to know her, and told both her and her parents that I'd love to come back whenever they needed me. We talked for a few more minutes, said goodbye, and then I made my way through the front door and past the huge saguaro cactus in their front yard to my vehicle, where I immediately pulled out my iPhone before turning the ignition switch. Still in the dark, as impatient as ever, I searched the internet for three words: Always be joyful.

Lighting up the driver's seat of my SUV, the blue screen read 1 Thessalonians 5:16–18. I knew that sounded familiar.

As I sat in my vehicle outside Bonnie's home, tears welled up in my eyes as I wondered, What just happened?

I began to realize that through my new friend Bonnie, God meant for me to learn something new and very important. I didn't know it yet, but this something—a Code, if you will—would affect me greatly. I began to think of it as The Bonnie Code.

Bonnie's Journal Entry #4, September 16

Hello,

Well, we are in the midst of trying to schedule surgery. The CT didn't show anything as far as the tunnel infection, but we knew it was a long shot to image the area anyway (so in this case not seeing anything doesn't mean nothing is there, it just means it wasn't able to be imaged this way). The CT did show that my lower abdominal cyst/fluid collection is still there and quite large, about the size of a large grapefruit, which probably helps account for the pain I have in that area. The echo didn't show any vegetation, which I was glad to hear, but given my persistent infection the ID (infection doc) wants a TEE done (which is a specialized echo, where they look at the heart from inside the chest, basically the same procedure as endoscopy).

The bad news ... another set of blood cultures showed up positive, which given that I've been on really strong IV antibiotics for over a month now should definitely NOT be happening. So, the port needs to come out, and sooner rather than later. Hopefully that will help get this infection under control (though, we also need to take a closer look at my heart, this the TEE). So, tomorrow (Monday) I am going into the hospital to have a venogram, to help us figure out if I can have a PICC line placed, or if I'll need a femoral line placed. They can't just take the old port out and immediately place a new one, they have to get the infected one out and then put in a temporary one, and then wait for several weeks until we can get the infection cleared, and then put the new port in (if they put the new one in right away it would just re-infect since the bacteria is in my blood stream).

. . . So there is a lot going on, and a lot ahead, and I don't even have the slightest idea of how it's all going to go down. As always my strategy is to just take one thing at a time, and trust that God has my back and has all of this already orchestrated. Prayers are ALWAYS appreciated, for me and my parents (and extended family, especially my brother who just left today for deployment in a combat zone). I will update more when I can, though I am gradually feeling worse and worse, so If I can't I'm sure Mummy will jump in.

This week is National Mitochondrial Disease Awareness Week, so please help spread the word!! This disease needs a treatment and a cure, but before we can even hope to get there we need more doctors and researchers to know that it exists!! Last week was Invisible Illness Awareness Week, and this is one of those invisible illnesses.

Thanks so much for all the thoughts and prayers, and thanks also for the guestbook entries, those are always really encouraging to me ☺

Love and Hugs,

Bonnie

5

Strength Through Weakness

"Three different times, I begged the Lord to take it away. Each time He said, 'My grace is all you need. My power works best in weakness.' So now I am glad to boast about my weaknesses, so that the power of Christ can work through me." **2 Corinthians 12:8–9** (New Living Translation)

After about six to seven months of visiting probably once or twice a month, I had learned a lot more about Bonnie Belle. Seeing photos of her at about ten years old, in her ballet dress and hovering high above the floor, her pointed toes one hundred and eighty degrees apart, made me realize that she was quite an athletic girl prior to the symptoms affecting her like they had. I couldn't help thinking about the freedoms that I personally have had—owning a small company that allowed me to play golf or tennis whenever I wanted or to go see a piano recital or sports event in the middle of the afternoon that one of my three kids was in.

I had prayed for Bonnie many times, often with my wife, Kimberly. I noticed though, that Bonnie didn't seem to be spending *her* time praying for healing.

Kimberly and I prayed, not only for Bonnie, but also for her parents, Dave and Lyn, who worked tirelessly around the clock, caring for *their* one and only favorite daughter. We prayed prayers of gratitude as well as for our health and the health of the five children that Kimberly and I have as our responsibility. It just didn't seem fair, though, that someone would have to lie in bed twenty-four seven, while we ran around doing whatever we wanted to. We knew this happened in every city in the world every day for many different reasons, but once you know someone personally and see and even feel their challenges and struggles, it is different and hits home to the very center of your heart.

I talked to Bonnie about her brother, Sean, who is a physician who has been deployed overseas and stateside. Sean and Bonnie had always been close, according to Bonnie and didn't get to see each other as often as they would like. With the success Dave and Lyn had raising Bonnie, I anticipated meeting Sean, assuming he would remind me of Bonnie, and I was correct. Sean was very sharp and had a similar sense of humor. Bonnie dearly loved her brother and spoke of him a lot. She particularly appreciated the 2014 Independence Day holiday that their entire family spent in Wells, Maine, with Bonnie's grandparents and Hurricane Arthur brought rain on July 4. Bonnie explained in a letter to me that they were able to watch fireworks from Moody Point and her note went on to say, "Even though it rained on the fourth, Sean put together a private pyrotechnic show for us with lots of sparklers and such; he got soaking wet as he ignited everything, but it was great!"

Bonnie loved the Northeast—staying at her grandparent's home, yelling for her beloved New England Patriots whenever they played. Recently, I was blessed to spend time with Bonnie's grandparents and parents, also huge Patriots fans. We watched the 2017 Super Bowl, as the Patriots pulled out that crazy game against the Atlanta Falcons. I told them upon arriving at their home that I was definitely yelling for the Falcons as the underdog, but they just smiled and strangely, I thought, didn't seem worried at all.

Bonnie's letters continued, sharing her favorite eating establishments. "Our favorite ice cream place up here for years has been Big Daddies—they have an amazing coffee heath flavor and even though we haven't had it as much as I would like, we have had it a few times. When I have my appointments in Boston in a couple of weeks, hopefully we will stop by Mike's. It's a great pastry shop in the north end and they have great cannoli's, lobster tails, and macaroons." Macaroons. Now we're talking.

Over many months, Bonnie and I talked about so many things: my kids; tennis tournaments, including one that I told my wife I would win for Bonnie and then gave Bonnie the trophy to prove it; movies; her grandparents; how her body was feeling and what tests were coming up; a trip to Stanford to see one of the top Mito docs; Christianity; Mallie; Christmas ornaments that she had received and given; how much Bonnie appreciated her parents love and expertise in nursing and the huge amount of time they spent taking care of her over the years. Bonnie and I would text often to share things that happened between personal visits. On one occasion, in June 2014, she sent me a text while she and her family were visiting her grandparents in Maine. She said her mummy was flying from Maine to Atlanta to attend a music seminar for a few days. Bonnie said in her text, "Dad and I will attempt to live without the 'glue' (Mummy) that holds everything together☺."

On another visit to Bonnie's home, we talked about what hymns we loved the most. That day, we simultaneously began singing together from memory:

"I stand amazed in the presence, of Jesus the Nazarene,

I wonder how He could love me, a sinner, condemned, unclean.

How marvelous, how wonderful, and my song, shall ever be, How marvelous, how wonderful is my Savior's love for me!"[11]

Bonnie told me about the time when she was about twelve years of age and her symptoms began to limit her activities more and more. She compared that time to her current time, at age thirty-one, and how difficult it was to shuffle between her home and doctor's offices or hospitals, often visiting physicians who did not understand mitochondrial diseases.

Bonnie had been confined to bed since she was about nineteen years old. Although she was admitted to the hospital with serious symptoms as a child, she would often be housed with adults since her physicians in Arizona did not know enough about Mito. Later, as she grew, some of the pediatric physicians began to learn more about Mito and, at twenty-one years old with her issues spiking, she found herself in a hospital bed at a children's hospital, watching the kids around her play with fun toys to make the time go by faster. She wondered aloud to me why she never had any fun things like that to spend time with when she was hospitalized as a youngster. Everything concerning her treatments seemed to be backwards.

One night, as I lay in bed unable to sleep, I couldn't help thinking about praying for Bonnie to have a free day to experience the things she could no longer experience. Again, it bothered me that I had the freedom to drive over to Monterey, California, and play the Pebble Beach golf course, or hop on a plane to Palm Springs and play tennis in a senior doubles tournament for four days. All the while, Bonnie was not only in bed, but couldn't go to the mall; couldn't ride her bike; couldn't jump on a plane and go see her grandparents in Maine; couldn't go to a movie theater; couldn't go out with friends; couldn't date and knew she would never have a child. Not only that, she was in constant pain and had to do regular blood transfusions, oxygen therapy, and a multitude of other daily tests, knowing that her situation was not going to get better. Yet, a smile and a prayer of gratitude was the response that she shared with others.

I want a free day for Bonnie and I am praying for it! I will trade one of mine for one of hers. I started praying that often and on one visit to Bonnie's, I told her about it. She, of course, was appreciative and showed that wide smile, but I could tell she did not take me seriously. Who would? A month or so later, sitting by her bedside, I told her that I was writing a story about her and in the story we did trade places for a day. I remember telling her dad that I was writing her story, but I don't think he thought I was serious, either. Finally, just after Christmas 2012, I told Bonnie and both her parents that they had better speak now if they did not want me to tell her story.

The fact is, I realized that Bonnie had done more good for the world, effected more people in a positive way, from her *bed*, twenty-four seven, in the last ten years, than I had on a regular basis with a healthy body over the past fifty years!

It was obvious what I was supposed to learn from this. The issue was when, or if, we would see some action on my part.

I was nudged again during my next visit to see Bonnie. Prior to leaving, she handed me a small slip of paper with the following written neatly on it: 2C129.

I had some guesses this time. When I arrived home, I figured it out. 2 Corinthians 12:9 (New Living Translation), "My grace is all you need. My power works best in weakness."

I thought to myself, Lord, thank you for this living example. What else do you have to show me?

Bonnie's Journal Entry #5, September 3

Hello. Well, I had my infectious disease appointment on Thursday, and it took a lot out of me. On the one hand, the doctor was pretty nice (turns out I had seen him before, as he had covered for another doctor one of the times I was admitted, and we both remembered each other, but I had only seen him briefly and he was never in charge of my case before), but what we learned in the visit turned out to be a little more unnerving than we were anticipating. The cultures had grown out a type of staph, and initially he thought that the clinical presentation with this tunnel infection was not usually typical of a staph bacteria (however, he isn't familiar with mito, and mito is known for not following a typical presentation), so he is more concerned that this tunnel infection could actually be a different type of infection, one more sinister, rare, and potentially harder to get rid of, and as a result wanted to get a CT scan of my chest, belly and pelvis to see if anything could be determined via imaging.

However, as we were about to leave, things changed. At the point I saw him I had been on strong antibiotics for over two weeks and had two sets of blood cultures done (one before starting the abx [antibiotics] and one after starting the abx), and a little over a day and a half before we saw him a third set was drawn to see how the abx were working. Even though it can be a little early for culture results to come back, at that point, we were hoping that maybe a preliminary report would be available for the doctor to see, though we were pretty much expecting them to be negative anyway since I had been on treatment for a while and it gets harder to get clear results when you're further into treatment (you can get false negatives). Just before we left the doc decided to check and see if a preliminary report had come in and turns out it had. The blood cultures were still POSITIVE!!! Not. Good.

So that changed things a bit. It's a hard balance, as we would like to be conservative with treatment when we can be, but we also need to be really aggressive when we need to be, and that is not only a hard line to balance, but also hard to get the doctors to understand that, as well. So far I think this doctor seems to understand that a little, but we've just seen him the one time and it's hard to know how he'll be long term.

So, that's the update so far. I can definitely tell that my body is dealing with/fighting something, so I'm trying to rest and not over-do so that it doesn't get worse and turn into full-on septic shock. Thank you so much for all of your prayers, I just don't know what is going to come of all this, and really, really don't want there to be any problems with my heart. Been there, done that, and don't want to do open heart surgery again! It's hard, but I continually try to rest in the Lord, knowing that He is all-powerful and all-knowing, and that He already knows how all of this will turn out. Once I know more I will update if I can, or if I'm not up to it probably Mummy will do it.

Please leave a note in the guestbook if you get a chance, the encouragement is definitely beneficial! ☺

Love and Hugs,

Bonnie ☺

6

SUBSTITUTION

"For they that wait upon the Lord shall renew their strength; they shall mount up with wings as eagles; they shall run and not be weary, and they shall walk and not faint." **Isaiah 40:31** (King James Version)

It was Saturday, April 6, 2013. The sound of xylophones from my iPhone brought me out of a deep slumber at exactly 6:30 a.m. I tried to reach over to turn off the alarm and could hardly move. I felt as though someone was holding me down. I opened my eyes to a blurry world. My head was pounding and my heart thumped quickly as though I had just finished a two hundred-meter sprint. Immediately, I said to myself, "What in the world is going on here?"

Twisting my body as hard as I could, I reached one arm out and turned off the alarm. Laying back on my pillow, I tried to yell, but it only came out in a slow, muffled, scratchy voice. "Kim-ber-ly!" No answer. So much for the 8:30 a.m. doubles matches this morning at Gene Autry Park.

For a moment, I thought maybe Kimberly had duct-taped my feet together or something for April Fool's Day, but then I remembered that April 1 had passed a few days earlier. Actually, this wasn't feeling funny at all.

Simultaneously, about ten miles away, my friend Bonnie Belle awoke from the best night of sleep that she can remember. She immediately felt so much more energetic and wondered aloud what was happening. Her eyesight and energy level were reminiscent of the last time she was performing on a gymnastics mat at about age ten. Bonnie fought the urge to pull out her oxygen line and multiple medical attachments as she yelled, "Mom! Dad! Come here, quick!"

Lyn and Dave were, of course, in panic mode and thought something was very wrong. They both came running—Dave pulling a shirt over his head as he ran into the room. Both stood in the den, a few feet away from Bonnie's bed, frozen and dumbfounded, to see such a healthy looking Bonnie with twinkling eyes and a huge smile on her face. They looked at each other, then back to Bonnie, then back to each other, three or four times before they could even speak. Tears began to flow from both parents' eyes as they grabbed Bonnie's body to keep her from trying to get out of bed.

"Bonnie, honey!" Lyn answered as she looked deep into Bonnie's eyes. "We need to make sure what we're doing before we do something stupid here. Let's slow down for a minute!"

"But, Mom! I feel amazing!"

Dave ran to get his phone, while Lyn wrapped her arms around Bonnie. Dave didn't even get through the open door, before bolting back and joining them both in a three-way hug fest. Bonnie quickly put her hand on her stomach and exclaimed, "I have absolutely no stomach pain and my head feels great! I need to get out of this bed! I'm hungry!"

Dave and Lyn traded silent stares again.

It was now 6:45 a.m.

Dave and Lyn both refused to let Bonnie remove her medical connections and told her that they needed to call Boston and get one of her doctors on the phone. It takes a while, especially on a Saturday, to get a couple of phone calls returned from Boston or Palo Alto. There was, of course, no rational, scientific explanation. There is no cure for Mito.

It was about 7:30 a.m., and Bonnie Belle had become Bouncing Belle. She finally talked her mom and dad into letting her remove herself from the tubes and monitoring devices long enough to make a quick trip to the bathroom. As Bonnie jumped out of bed, she caused the butterflies hanging from her ceiling to float around with glee. "Wow! This is awesome!" Bonnie shrieked, as she got to the bathroom, leaned over the sink and looked at her face in the mirror from about six inches away. Quietly, she mused, "How long has it been since I've been able to do this?"

Bonnie found Mallie—actually, the dog found her—and hugged Mallie so tightly that it put the pup in a panic. Mallie jumped out of Bonnie's arms, running wildly around the house, that leash whipping around behind her, leaving scars on the furniture.

Bonnie grabbed a pair of tennis shoes from the homemade stepstool beside her bed. This was no ordinary stepstool, mind you, but one that her mummy made to double as a storage device. That Lyn was pretty crafty. I would say the stepstool had approximately the same storage capacity as your average refrigerator. Bonnie reached down, tied her shoes, and walked calmly to the front door of the house, looking back tentatively to see if her mom and dad were watching. Dave was on the phone and Lyn was looking around the French doors of the den, wondering what in the world Bonnie would do next.

Bonnie didn't give them much time to wonder, as she bolted out the front screen door and stood on the sidewalk next to the stately saguaro cactus in their front yard, her arms raised high and her face pointed to the sky. She stopped, silently breathed deep for five or six seconds, then lowered her arms, turned, and sprinted west down the sidewalk. Lyn ran quickly to peer through the front windows, wiping away tears and hoping to watch her without being seen.

Bonnie sprinted like a gazelle down the sidewalk, around the cul-de-sac about a block away, then back down the street toward her home. In the neighbor's driveway, there was a hopscotch game drawn in colored chalk and Bonnie navigated it perfectly, first with one foot, then the other, then both together—the most amazing smile across her face.

Arriving back at her front porch, she grabbed her dad's bike and took off east on it toward the school. Lyn lost sight of Bonnie and ran to her cell phone to call the grandparents and give them the unbelievable news. Dave was now on the phone trying to reach Bonnie's brother, Sean. Any neighbors who were up on that Saturday morning could hear Bonnie sing at the top of her lungs, "I stand, amazed in the presence," as she rode down the street.

As Bonnie parked the bike a few minutes later, she hesitated a moment on the front porch, going through several memories of her life—from her five year old ballet class, to birthday parties, swimming, visits to the ocean, then memories of being at the hospital, very ill, for months at a time. After what seemed like ten minutes of memories flashing through her head, she realized she was daydreaming and pinched her own arm, jumped up and down, and then ran in the house to look in the mirror again.

"Oh, my goodness! Is this real?"

Bonnie heard her parents from different parts of the house trying to describe the events of the last hour to different people, in tears and full of joy. They continued peeking around the corner to get a quick look at Bonnie, then ducking back in to speak in relative quiet tones again on the phone.

Bonnie simultaneously grabbed her cell phone in her left hand and sat down at a table typing on her laptop with right hand, trying to tell as many people as possible about the incredible news.

In the meantime, I, without Bonnie knowing, was struggling more and more and could not get out of bed. Kimberly called 911 and they arrived at our home. The EMTs and Kimberly believed I was in dire trouble, but I stayed awake and stable on the way to the hospital. The ambulance took me to the hospital where Dave worked and where Bonnie had been locally treated on many occasions over the past seventeen years.

My mind began searching through a series of memories of my own childhood, school, music, and sports. This feeling was very new to me. I had never experienced anything even remotely like this.

Bonnie, meanwhile, was still at the computer and had been busy calling, texting, and emailing as many folks as she could think of. She came to a list that she and Lyn had made with the names of people whom had come to Bonnie-sit over the past few years. Going down the list, she read Sarah Moore, Elizabeth Tompkins, Leilany Mamoe, then came across my name. Her face changed from unbridled joy to horror as she remembered the story and prayers I had told her about. She frantically dialed my cell phone number and got a voice mail message. My phone sat on my bedside table at home while I was on my way to the hospital.

Bonnie ran to her parents, frightening them with the look on her face. As she explained the story that I told her, her parents listened, but were in obvious disbelief. Bonnie asked her parents if they knew where I lived and they confessed they did not, but that the Compassion Ministries coordinators, Joy and Abe, would probably know. Dialing Abe and Joy's number, they all jumped in the car. They arrived at my home about fifteen minutes later. They rang the doorbell, but no one answered.

Dave called the three closest emergency rooms to see if anyone had come in with strange symptoms like what I may be experiencing. The third one he tried was his place of work, and they verified an ambulance had brought a man fitting my description and symptoms. Back to the car they went.

Upon arriving at the hospital, they found Kimberly and I. Bonnie was in tears as she saw me for the first time in my condition and saw the pain on my face. It was as if I had aged ten years since I last visited her two weeks earlier. It was so strange to see her looking so healthy and moving everywhere so quickly. As she entered the emergency room area, a couple of ER employees looked closely at Bonnie, then exchanged glances, apparently thinking, Don't we know her?

Bonnie walked immediately to my bedside and grabbed my hand. My wife had my other one. As I felt both hands being squeezed, my eyes opened, then slowly moved to Bonnie and a smile came over my pained face. A tear slowly ran down my cheek and Kimberly, Bonnie, Dave, and Lyn shared in my emotion.

My three children began showing up at the hospital, my oldest, Bradley, still on his way from Denver. Korey and Tommy walked right over to join us, but were told there were too many people in my room and they'd have to take turns.

Somewhat in shock, they were each very quiet, running flashbacks in their own minds of growing up, competing with their dad in a variety of sports (they say I almost never let them win), as well as remembering the emotion, the doubt, and the lack of understanding that came with watching their parents struggle through a divorce. Mainly, they seemed to be thinking, What is going on here?

My kids have almost never seen me ill. In serious pain and discomfort, a discomfort that I never would have imagined someone could experience twenty-four seven for years, and with my eyes closed I thought back to telling my kids multiple times that if offered the chance to do those painful years over again, I would *not* choose divorce, no matter what. I remember telling them I was so sorry for leaving them and their home during their important junior high and high school years. Another pain I experienced was not knowing whether they had truly ever forgiven me.

The hustle and bustle noises of the emergency department shook me out of those thoughts, and I flashed back to the visual of Bonnie riding her bike this morning down the street, singing at the top of her lungs. I felt a smile slowly form on my lips. I took a deep breath, exhaled, and suddenly woke up in my bed at home, with my wife, Kimberly, shaking my arm.

"What in the world were you talking about?" Kimberly questioned, her eyeballs twice their normal size. I looked down at my arms and legs, at my surroundings, back at Kimberly, and then up at the ceiling, where I silently voiced a question to the Lord. "So that was your way of allowing me to trade places for a day, huh? You're kidding me."

Immediately, my mind went back to Bonnie. I was horrified, thinking of the unbridled joy she experienced in my dream, only to realize that what I had imagined was apparently not in God's plan.

I asked Kimberly to give me five minutes and began to think about my true yearning for the chance to be able to give Bonnie a day to experience freedom again.

My mind began to wander to some historical examples of substitution and sacrifice. This single thought, after all, was what initially fueled the deep feelings of compassion for Bonnie, as I watched her physical situation degrade over time. As I told Kimberly earlier, I truly would trade places with Bonnie *if* I knew there was a chance she could have a full life. I was now fifty-four, with my kids raised and old enough to be out on their own. Bonnie was thirty-one. This hypothetical scenario would not be fair to Kimberly, but she understood my comment and my feelings. Those who know my wife know that she is an incredibly gifted, giving person.

My mind drifted back again to those examples of historical substitution and sacrifice, beginning with the most obvious, Jesus Christ, following through with a plan devised prior to the creation of the earth by dying on the cross for the sins of humanity, then rising on the third day, offering eternal life for all who believe in Him and ask Him into their heart. The Ultimate Sacrifice.

Next, I hearkened back, not so far this time, to high school and a novel written by Charles Dickens called *A Tale of Two Cities*, in which an incarcerated criminal named Sydney Carton devised and implemented a plan to switch clothes with a prisoner who was awaiting execution. Carton pulls it off and goes to the guillotine that day, dying for the other man. His actions created a certain paradox—that Carton achieved a better life through death than through anything he could have ever done for the remaining portion of his life in prison. This action enabled him to live on, at least in the positive memory of others, and allowed him to perform one meaningful act in his life before his death, bringing those famous peaceful thoughts from Carton: "It is a far, far better rest than I go to than I have ever known." [12]

Third, and even more recently, I remembered a college sports story about Tom Walter, the Wake Forest baseball coach, donating one of his kidneys to one of his new players, Kevin Jordan, at the start of Coach Walter's second season in 2011, about the same time I met Bonnie. Coach Walter spoke about his player. "We talk about taking ownership. Here's a young man who took ownership. He moved away from home with this condition, checked into his dorm room, hooked himself up to a dialysis machine, and fought for his life every single day. I had to help. I had to help. It was a no-brainer."[13] This was an amazing story of sacrifice from a man who, by all reports, lives character, integrity, and family.

I'm reminded of one additional sacrifice. My wife and I have hosted a Bible study at our home for the past nine years. One of our eighteen or so friends and attendees, Marci Hall, recently donated one of her kidneys. Though not in the national limelight, this act is of equal sacrifice and was such an example of love. We are so blessed to have Marci and her husband, Jim, as our close friends and compassion-givers. If you have thought about joining a group of believers or hosting a group at your own home, but just haven't done so, go right ahead and act on it!

By no means, by the way, am I comparing the importance and significance to our world and to God's plan of the ultimate sacrifice of Jesus Christ and His subsequent resurrection to these other examples of sacrifice—one fictional, three true. Just want to be clear.

My five minutes were up, and I needed to get out of bed. Kimberly wanted some answers as to why I was apparently making strange noises in my sleep. I told her that my prayers were answered for Bonnie—at least for a short time in my mind. I told Kimberly that physically, the dream was a nightmare, but the visions of Bonnie in it were literally a dream come true. My heart was still pounding. As I swung my feet off the bed, my mind thought about Bonnie and how her compassionate heart had touched so many.

Bonnie's Journal Entry #6, April 20

Hello,

I thought I would post a very brief note, just to say hi and wish everyone a joyous Easter. ☺ I will update more about me a little later, but it has been a really crazy few months, the theme could be "one thing after another." My grandparents are leaving Arizona today to head back to Maine, and I am very sad to see them go. Next to my parents, they are the people I see the most (and for whatever reason I have very few other visitors), and one good thing about my illness is that it has allowed me to spend time with them (they "Bonnie-sit" a bunch) ☺ and we have a close, special relationship. So, I think when they leave it will be a teary goodbye.

Many Easter blessings to all of you. I think the following hymn verse sums it up well:

Jesus paid it all, all to Him I owe;

Sin had left a crimson stain, he washed it white as snow!

He is risen! Happy Resurrection Day!

Love and Hugs,

Bonnie ☺

7

THE DOUBLE H

"Even though the fig trees have no blossoms and there are no grapes on the vines; even though the olive crop fails and the fields lie empty and barren; even though the flocks die in the fields and the cattle barns are empty—yet, I will rejoice in the Lord! I will be joyful in the God of my salvation!" **Habakkuk 3:17–18** (New Living Translation)

H abakkuk? How do you even pronounce that? Maybe like sitting duck? Bacchic? Megabuck? At least one of these makes a nice segue for this chapter. My Redemption Church friend, Neil Pitchel, who happens to know just *slightly* more than I do about the Old Testament, the Hebrew and Greek languages, the Jewish culture , and pretty much everything else, says that the emphasis is on the middle syllable, if that helps.

Habakkuk, seventh century B.C. prophet, in the process of lodging a verbal complaint with God, just comes right out and asks the Lord, "Surely you don't plan to allow the Babylonians to wipe us out?" Habakkuk then continues, without waiting for an answer, moving his question into the negotiation stage: "Should you be silent while the wicked swallow up people more righteous than they? Are we only fish to be caught and killed?"[14]

Habakkuk then informs the Creator of the universe that he, Habakkuk, was going to climb up to his watchtower and stand at his guard post to have the best view to watch and wait for God's answer to him. It didn't take long and, unlike a common scenario for people waiting high up in a guard post, the answer didn't come by runner.

Unfortunately, the Lord's answer initially made Habakkuk *feel* like a sitting duck. He spoke to Habakkuk about those who are proud— the lovers of money, the arrogant, dishonest, and corrupt people— and yes, those who commit evil. The Lord warned all those people by saying, "What sorrows await you."[15]

The Lord went on to add idol creation[16] to this list – trusting in things we make as humans and things we simply make too important. Sometimes we forget that idols can be good things, like our family, our job, our children, or a hobby. Even though these things are normally good things, they can separate us from God's design for us, which is to worship Him. As humans, we are good at worshipping, aren't we? Worshipping *something*, anyway.

An important part of the discussion of Habakkuk is that the Lord warned him in the Bible that humans will encounter evil and injustice for a time. Good people who put their trust in God will be discouraged, afraid, and even fearful, as we watch what is happening in our world right now. Yet, to read Habakkuk's prayer[17] (He sang it, by the way. I'd like to have a CD of that performance, from around 600 B.C.), we realize that Habakkuk truly trusted God to ultimately take care of those who are faithful to Him and those who are willing to wait for what He has to say to us. Habakkuk thanked the Lord for answering his complaint and his questions, and Habakkuk's heart of trust was revealed, as he stated in chapter 3, verses 17–19 (New Living Translation). "Even though the fig trees have no blossoms and there are no grapes on the vines; even though the olive crop fails and the fields lie empty and barren; even though the flocks die in the fields and the cattle barns are empty—yet, I will rejoice in the Lord! I will be joyful in the God of my salvation! The sovereign Lord is my strength! He makes me as surefooted as a deer, able to tread on the heights."

If only we could keep our hearts this true and trusting in the face of danger, in the face of heartbreak, illness, job loss, addiction, family breakups, cancer diagnoses, discomfort, pain, and suffering.

After hearing the Habakkuk story a few times in my life, I now have a new and real-life example of the Double-H. What is the Double-H? The Habakkuk Heart, of course. My example was—you guessed it— Bonnie Codier.

Instead of a loss of food, oil, crops, and flocks, Bonnie Belle experienced over many years, twenty-four seven, a loss of normal human function: normal heart function, normal lung function, normal digestive function, the ability to hop in the car with friends and go to a movie theater or church, the loss of ever being able to date, to marry or to have children—all a loss of things that most of us take daily for granted! And yet, Bonnie not only paralleled the Double-H of "Yet, I will rejoice in the Lord!", Bonnie truly *lived* it, by example and bedridden through her CaringBridge site, phone calls, texts, Facebook, and, of course, in person to those blessed to meet her.

Did Bonnie ever lodge a complaint with God himself? According to her, she absolutely did! She wouldn't be human, otherwise. She wrestled with the responsibility of accepting her pain and discomfort—a task handed to her at a young age. Bonnie told me she finally asked the Lord this question: "Which way will I be able to serve you better, Lord—traveling as a world-class dancer? Or from a bed? Your call, Lord. You know I'm with you, either way."

Sitting quietly by her bed, watching those butterflies slowly dancing in the air above her, I listened to her tell me about this conversation she had with the Holy Spirit, and tears flowed from my eyes just as they are at this moment. At the time, I could almost not read the slip of paper that she reached out and handed me with the following written on it: H31718. "Yet, I will rejoice in the Lord."

Of the almost four years that I knew Bonnie personally, I believe that she was beyond the point where she might pray for God's healing of her body. Not that she didn't believe He *could*, just that she knew by that time His plan for her was for her to be exactly where she was. I never once heard a word of self-pity emanate from Bonnie Belle. She never once asked me to pray for her healing. We did, however, pray for others—her brother, Sean; her parents; my wife and our children; our jobs; her grandparents; her friends going through similar Mito battles; all the people out there who live alone or are disabled and can't get out of the house to hear God's Word shared in person; even prayers for those who had hurt us, whether with deeds or just with words.

These prayers tended to bring both of us to a thankful state of mind, a state that has a way of violently pushing the selfishness out of our living rooms, out of our vehicles and out of our work cubicles. It reminds me of a quote by Michael Ward, University of Oxford professor, given in his commencement speech to the students of Hillsdale College in May of 2015. He said, "The important thing is not to be in a certain state, but to be a certain kind of person in whichever state you find yourself."[18]

Powerful. Enough wisdom here that I suppose Habakkuk would probably have been happy to make this statement himself. Maybe he did.

THE CODE

Jesus replied, "You must love the Lord your God with all your heart, all your soul and all your mind. This is the first and greatest commandment. A second is equally important: Love your neighbor as yourself. The entire law and all the demands of the prophets are based on these two commandments." **Matthew 22:37–40** (New Living Translation)

A few years ago, a family friend of ours, author Kally Reynolds, told me that she thought I should write a story about a father's love for his daughter. She knew about my divorce with the mother of my one and only favorite daughter, Korey, and she knew how it hurt me to look back and realize the devastation that this divorce caused my family. I thought her story idea was a good one and I told her I might do that someday.

As I began to write this story, I remembered Kally's recommendation, and I realized that the Bonnie Codier story *is* about a father's love for his daughter. It actually describes three fathers and the love that each one has for his daughter.

First, the love and caring sacrifice that David Codier provided to his daughter, Bonnie, for years and years, with his wife, Lyn, by his side. They traded nurse shifts at home when their own personal energy meters were on empty in the middle of the night, as they both had worked hard all day and yet, Bonnie moaned in pain and discomfort. The intricate oxygen setup to her bedside; elaborate electronic and audio-visual installations that Dave designed and installed to allow Bonnie to be as comfortable as possible. The homemade stairway/shoe storage unit that Lyn designed and that allowed Bonnie's favorite canine, Mallie, to climb up and snuggle with her in bed any time of the day or night. A request by Dave and Lyn to the Compassion Team for additional Bonnie-sitters—a request that allowed more people, including myself, the blessing of knowing Dave, Lyn, Bonnie, and Sean, while offering some degree of respite for the Codier family. These are just a few examples of a father's love.

Second, the love and concern that I had instinctively grabbing my daughter's ankle while scuba diving in the Gulf of Mexico and pulling her back down to me to save her lungs in the midst of the panic of dozens of painful jellyfish stings. The love that a father has, being able to share an activity like this with his daughter. The love that I feel when Korey takes time out of her busy day to share a meal with me, or watch a movie with me and laugh with me.

Any father of a daughter knows the horrible feeling that comes over us when the bond is broken between us, especially when we had something to do with that break. In my particular case, leaving my daughter and her two brothers without a father at home during their junior high and high school years haunted me for a long time and still does. If it were not for my Heavenly Father's forgiveness, grace and mercy, I would continue being haunted forever for leaving them, no matter what the reason for leaving was. I can only hope that my children, especially my daughter, will fully forgive me that choice, as I know that it still bothers us both, even as I know God has forgiven me. If there is a father out there reading this that is thinking about divorce, I plead with you to turn away from that thought. There is help out there!

Korey did allow me a very special moment a few years ago as I was visiting northwestern Michigan with my wife, Kimberly; standing by myself for just a few minutes on a small flat spot on the Sleeping Bear Sand Dunes, south of Traverse City, overlooking the wonderfully vast Lake Michigan to the north and west. (By the way, did you know that place was voted the most beautiful place in America in 2011?) I gazed at the majesty of this area and God's Creation on a sunny day in August. I watched people roll down the four hundred fifty foot tall sand dunes from the pinnacle to the beach, then rise to their feet, turn around, and take the arduous side-to-side hike back up, only to purposefully fall down and do it again, sand infiltrating their constant smiles. Standing there in surprising quiet on that August day with just a light breeze ruffling my hair, my cell phone buzzed to indicate a text had arrived. My first thought was, Is there really a cell tower near here? I plucked the phone out of my pocket, took off my sunglasses, shaded the screen from the glaring sun, and there, on my phone, was a text from my daughter, Korey. I had not heard from her in what I estimated to be about two years.

The love I had for my daughter and the timing of this event brought tears before I could even read the text. She said, in essence, that she had been thinking about God's forgiveness for her and that she felt she should and would forgive me, as well. That did it. Now I couldn't even see the lake.

Korey is a great singer. You can believe that statement, even though it is her proud father stating the fact. She asked me to send one of her renditions of an acapella Christmas song to Bonnie during Christmas 2014, and I did so. Bonnie told me she listened to "Have Yourself a Merry Little Christmas" many times while praying for Korey and for my relationship with Korey. Bonnie was so appreciative of that gift and was verbally supportive in believing that over time, I would see my relationship with Korey be fully restored. In fact, here are Bonnie's actual comments from her December 2014 texts: "Is that her singing?" (yes) "Wow ... that is incredible! She has a beautiful voice! Please thank her so much 4 me!!"

Neither of these fatherly examples, however, compare to the love shown by our Father God in heaven, who has been in constant and direct communication through prayer and through the Holy Spirit with Dave and Lyn's little Bonnie Belle for many years as she dealt with her physical battle, ultimately trusting in Him through it all. Even now, in personal contact, as Bonnie dances in praise to Him. Bonnie's Heavenly Father loved her with a divine love—a love that provided Bonnie with that true joy that we hear of and sometimes even participate in. A joy that humans in pain and suffering don't draw from naturally.

Thank you, Lord, for the Father's love that you have shown to Bonnie, to Dave, and to me, and for the example that you have given us of how to love our daughters, even as we do so imperfectly!

We lost Bonnie on Tuesday, February 10, 2015, in the middle of the day. I remember the phone call coming in, preceded by a quick text from Bonnie's dad asking if I was in my office and if he could call me. I knew Bonnie had been in the battle of her life for the past few days, and my wife and I had been preparing ourselves mentally for this moment.

I hadn't been able to visit Bonnie for about three weeks due to an upper respiratory issue that I didn't want to share with her, her family, or anyone at the hospital. Bonnie had her entire extended family at the hospital ICU with her. Prior to the decision to intubate, which is where they place a flexible plastic tube into the windpipe to maintain an open airway, and go on a ventilator, she personally wrote out a page and a half of instructions for her family and the physicians and nursing staff.

Most of the instructions were living will-related, like, "I want to continue the fight for a couple of days." One instruction, however, had to do with a physician who was currently working with her while not realizing that, years ago, he had gone through some tentative and stressful moments with a family about hospital care and physician knowledge, or the lack of it, relating to a mitochondrial patient in his care. Bonnie's written instructions were something like, "Make sure you are positioned close to Dr. X's face when he finally realizes that the patient and family he was working with back then was us!"

My employer happens to be one of the top handful of health care Integrated Delivery Networks, or IDNs, in the United States. An IDN is a health care system with multiple hospitals, clinics, research centers, academic centers, behavioral health facilities, home care, urgent care, and/or other providers that work together on different levels to improve the population health of a geographic area. Since I do work in this industry and since I do believe strongly in the skills, abilities, and the general level of compassion that is evident in our people, it seems a bit strange for me to infer that physician knowledge of a particular subject, mitochondrial disease in this case, is less than desired. However, I believe Bonnie's story illuminates this fact and hopefully will help to change it for the better in the years to come. The fact that Bonnie, in her extremely weakened state, had to be driven to either Boston, Massachusetts, or Palo Alto, California, to see a specialist is one example. To fly Bonnie to Boston from Phoenix in her state of health was quoted at around $12,000.

There are a few examples of patient care breakdowns at multiple health care companies and health care facilities across multiple states that I'd like to mention, for Bonnie and her family's sake—mainly to remind all of us in the health care field that although caregivers are human and there will always be human error, we must focus on continual improvement and remember that everything we do during our time on the job affects a life, good or bad, and even by those of us who do not provide direct patient care.

- At sixteen years of age, Bonnie went in for a laparoscopic splenectomy (spleen removal), at which time her pancreas was nicked, resulting in a full abdominal surgery to remove the spleen and control the bleeding. The spleen was then mishandled in post-op pathology and the organ ended up useless to examine. The cause of the initial issue was never found, resulting in delayed diagnosis and continued frustration for her family.

- That same year and prior to Mito diagnosis, a muscle biopsy was done, but the slides were lost, delaying her diagnosis further.

- After Mito diagnosis, at age twenty-nine, another biopsy was taken and was also lost.

There were definitely other issues and misunderstandings, but Bonnie and her parents made the best of what they had.

Remembering a visit with Bonnie in early 2014, there was a moment that I thought she was going to ask me to pray for her situation, then realized that she was asking that I pray about Lyn, her mummy, as Bonnie called her. I had heard whispers earlier from some of the Compassion Team that Lyn had lost some weight and was experiencing some symptoms of late-onset mitochondrial disease. I spoke aloud, "Are you kidding me?"

I began noticing Lyn's weight loss myself and began talking about it with Lyn and Dave. On one visit to their home, Lyn beamed excitedly and pointed to the corner of the room, saying, "Check out my new wheelchair!" Like Bonnie, Lyn was not known to complain.

When Lyn attended Bonnie's Celebration of Life in her new wheelchair, it was somewhat of a surprise to me. Indeed, Lyn confided that she had lost over thirty pounds of muscle. What now? Why? How was Dave taking this?

What an opportunity to be angry with God, whether you are a Bible-believer or not! If you are not a believer in God, maybe just an opportunity to be angry and show frustration in your circumstances? Again, like Bonnie and Lyn, Dave seemed to resist the temptation to be angry. With his nursing background and firsthand knowledge of mitochondrial disease, he was aware of the chance of late-onset Mito. And, knowing Dave as I do, I'm sure he is of the belief that having a personal relationship with the Creator of the universe does not guarantee that the Lord will never allow difficult events in our lives. I've never heard Dave complain about the many difficulties his family has experienced.

Bonnie's family would tell you that they are definitely not alone in their feelings of suffering and loss and how they have dealt with it. In fact, I know they are not alone, as we have multiple sets of mutual friends whose families are going through suffering. Here are just a few examples.

- Kevin and Kim: Kevin was a successful commercial real estate broker and, having played golf with him, I believe he was about a 2-handicap golfer. Just a few years ago, he suffered multiple strokes and some cancer scares, leaving the left half of his body paralyzed. His mind is not paralyzed, though, as he continues to, along with his strong, courageous, and Spirit-filled wife, rejoice in the Lord and witness with a smile to his caregivers and anyone else they meet.

Kevin and Kim have two loving, helpful sons, Spencer and Tyler, who have been supportive of their time and encouragement. They're another example of a couple that, in the midst of suffering, continue to provide incredible blessings, as opposed to asking for one. We love to spend time with them in the cool pines of Arizona.

- Abe and Joy: Since Joy introduced me to the Codier family in 2011, her husband Abe has more recently suffered a stroke and multiple complications, resulting in a recent ICU stay in 2016 of almost four months, being in and out of the hospital for a year, and not being able to swallow for most of this time. During one visit my wife and I made to their home, Abe was mostly excited to tell us how, while teaching his brain to function again, his brain forgot that his left leg had been damaged by back surgery eleven years prior and is now working again! His favorite words during this severe season of suffering are, "Praise the Lord!" Joy's name describes her to a T. Her CaringBridge posts from these challenging times could easily make up a Bible study guide for faith, perseverance, and trust in Jesus for people involved in the daily, common tests of our faith.

- Gary and Adrienne: Gary and Adrienne were married for fifty-three years, with Adrienne holding down the fort as the Biblical believer for about the first forty of them. Gary's travels took him from the Marines to engineer of aircraft engines to counterterrorism work across the globe, but it was an automobile accident and a broken neck a few years ago that made him think twice about life and whether Jesus's life, death, and resurrection meant anything to him. With some time to think, he decided that Jesus's gifts mean everything. Adrienne was diagnosed with leukemia a few years later and struggled with the difficulties of a bone marrow transplant, shingles, and new energy limits that changed both of their lives. Although very much a challenge, these unplanned and unexpected occurrences changed their faith in Christ for the better. Gary continued to model the Ephesians 5:25 instruction that husbands are to love their wives as Christ loves the Church, and has been such a great example of this to all who know him. We lost Adrienne to her illness about a year beyond her physician's estimate of her body's ability to endure. Gary, his extended family, and all of us who knew Adrienne, especially my wife, Kimberly, looked at this additional year as a true gift.

- Curtis and Angela: I'm not sure if the title "Ground Zero for Compassion and Counseling at Redemption Church" would be accepted by these two, but I'll use it, because I have the pen. They have four lovely daughters, and one of them, Tiana, has struggled for years with serious medical issues, in and out of the hospital and treatment. Through it, these two have shown and continually show the love of Jesus and a faithfulness to Him that is such an example to so, so many people. I know my wife and I have learned so much from these dear friends of ours who are also mentors to many.

Kimberly and I have other examples of friends that show amazing grace during the testing of their faith, with some heart-wrenching stories of suffering. We recently finished a home group study of Hebrews, using the *John MacArthur New Testament Commentary on Hebrews*, in which the author shared a very fitting comment, especially as an answer to a common question we hear in this world today. "Why does God allow such pain to afflict good people?"

An apparent common expectation is that if a person puts his or her faith in God, they should not have to deal with physical pain and suffering. Pastor MacArthur explains, "God's rest is not essentially physical at all ... The rest God promises is spiritual, not physical." He goes on to say, "Some of God's most faithful believers are the busiest, the hardest working, and sometimes the most afflicted people imaginable. Yet, they are in God's salvation rest."[19]

For another example of a person dealing with the question of how God can allow tragedy to affect someone who believes in and loves Him positively, check out the book *A Grace Disguised* by Jerry Sittser. You will not be disappointed.

Speaking of affliction and rest in the same paragraph, I wanted to share an update on Bonnie's mother, Lyn. After Bonnie's passing in 2015, Lyn continued to struggle with the Mito she dealt with all her life, but a Mito that had intensified over the past three years. Lyn finally succumbed to this long battle on February 26, 2018, when she joined Bonnie in heaven.

In addition to homeschooling Bonnie and Sean as they grew up, Lyn taught hundreds of young children and their parents the joy of music, its developmental benefits, and how it can teach us about God and bring us closer to Him in worship.

During those last months and weeks of Lyn's battle, my wife, Kimberly, and I enjoyed some beautiful moments with Lyn: Kimberly lying in bed with her, lightly caressing her hair and hands, while I kneeled beside her bed and laughed at Lyn's amazing stories, as well as her effervescent sense of humor. Kimberly called Lyn "the smartest lady I've ever known."

By the way, this is only a brief note on Lyn and definitely does not do her legacy justice, but if you've noticed the true joy in Bonnie's life through this story, Lyn instilled much of that through her teaching and her living example.

During those last couple of visits, Lyn told Kimberly and me about her miracle kids. She knew going into marriage that she had symptoms of mitochondrial disease and may not be able to have children. Therefore, when she became pregnant with her son, Sean, she initially, in her words, "thought I had developed a cyst in my abdomen." Sean proved that incorrect. By the time Lyn became pregnant with Bonnie, she obviously knew that pregnancy was possible. As soon as she found out it was a girl, she said, "I immediately went out and bought a little dress."

Doctors were worried about the birth and the health of both Lyn and Bonnie, so they did not want her to go to full-term in her pregnancy. Lyn told us that she and Dave utilized a midwife, who in Lyn's words " ... literally pushed Bonnie out."

I don't know who this midwife was, but I'm *so* thankful for you!

Bonnie Codier changed my life. I was always a nice, helpful guy and a fairly compassionate person. But I was one that often found a reason why I didn't have time during a given week to share that compassion with others. Thanks to my mom, I had heard of God, Jesus Christ, and the Holy Spirit since before I was old enough to write those words. Yet, I can confidently tell you that I have not practiced the commandment to "Love the Lord with all my heart, soul, mind, and strength—and to love my neighbor as I do myself"[20] as much in half a century and a healthy body as Bonnie did, bedridden, from the time she was twenty-one to thirty-one years of age.

That was the most important Code that Bonnie shared with me. For this one, she didn't hand me a piece of paper—she simply proved it from the time I met her until the Lord took her home. I imagine you've heard Matthew 22:37–39 called "The Great Commandment." I had heard it, but Bonnie lived it. Because of Bonnie, I am more focused on this than ever before.

Another of the Bonnie Codes was 2 Corinthians 12:9, which says that God's grace is all we need. His power works best in weakness. Bonnie was the best example of this that I've ever seen, with her mom and the other couples' examples I gave just a page or two ago, right behind her.

As mentioned in chapter seven, Bonnie taught me to rejoice in the Lord no matter my circumstances (Habakkuk 3). It is a lesson desperately needed in today's world.

Last, Bonnie taught me to always be thankful and to pray more, and Bonnie's example helped me to be more thankful, no matter my circumstances. I am now better at it and continue to strive to improve.

I will obviously never forget Bonnie Codier and her wisdom and courage. She has been the best example to me of the fruit of the Spirit from Galatians 5:22 (New Living Translation). "But the Holy Spirit produces this kind of fruit in our lives: love, joy, peace, patience, kindness, goodness, faithfulness, gentleness, and self-control. There is no law against these things."

Years ago, I kept a sticky note on my car dashboard with the fruits listed on it to remind me to test myself on each one often. The note brought a few good discussions as my kids asked me about the list. Unfortunately, I usually wouldn't get very far without realizing I had some work to do on each one of these.

Every once in a while, I would see the fruit in my kids and would remember how it forms and affects our actions. One Sunday morning several years back, my kids and I parked a long distance from the church entrance in the road to the west of the large parking lot. Between that road and the parking lot was a rock-filled ditch that my daughter was having a difficult time traversing in some cool heels and the dress she was wearing. My oldest son, Bradley, immediately recognizing her plight, quickly picked Korey up in his arms, walked her across the ditch, and put her down gently on the other side.

I didn't think much about the gesture, but the next morning, I visited a bagel shop near there that I had never been to before. As I was looking up at the menu high on the wall, I got that feeling I was being stared at. I looked at the cashier to place my order and, before I could speak, she immediately asked, "Do you and your family go to Redemption Church?" Stunned, as I didn't know her and had not been in the bagel shop before, I smiled and responded that we sure did. She replied, "Yesterday was the first time my family and I had ever attended there, and we saw you and how your son helped your daughter. If the teaching there has that kind of result on children, that's the church we want to attend."

We just never know when our kids or we might take some action that will touch someone's life, do we? It could be simply getting to know someone and showing love to them or their family. To me, this behavior reminds me of the term sympathetic resonance. Like a tuning fork or the strings of a piano or guitar that vibrate and affect other strings near them and add richness, people's loving actions can and do provide richness in a difficult world. My son's actions that day had a positive effect on another family. And Bonnie's ability to take her focus off her everyday battle and move her smiles, joy, and encouragement to assist others who were struggling, brought a richness that affected hundreds of thousands of people on the internet and many people locally, and definitely changed one life for the better—mine.

I once read a comment by Pastor Greg Laurie of Harvest Christian Fellowship who said, "I believe my job as a Pastor is to comfort the afflicted—and to afflict the comfortable."[21]

I printed and carried that post in my briefcase for several years, along with a few others of Pastor Laurie's, reading them often. Another one that hit home was his question, "What's Your Excuse?" Pastor Laurie continued, "A lot of times we will come up with excuses as to why God cannot use us. Maybe it is a fear of public speaking ... Others might think God could never use me, because I am not a professional. But that is probably an asset, not a liability. If you can be an authentic Christian who knows your Bible and who is able to articulate the gospel message, you would be amazed at what God could do through you ... IF you would be willing to take a step of faith."

Greg Laurie's words from those posts, other messages from his radio show, and the truths that my family and friends hear on a regular basis from our nondenominational Bible church definitely afflicted me right out of my comfort zone. Enough, I think, to take that first step toward answering that email and ultimately visiting the Codier home on that Sunday back in April, 2011.

Exactly five months and eleven days prior to Bonnie's passing in 2015, Kimberly and I joined Bonnie and her parents for what was to be an informal dinner on and around their living room sofa. It ended up being four hours of dinner, storytelling, and laughter that we will never forget. It was also four hours of energy consumption for Bonnie that would no doubt, take her two or three days to catch up on. At one point during that time together, in the middle of a serious attempt to explain to Bonnie and her parents what she meant to me, I noticed that their sofa pillows all had lighthouses on them. In my usual, bumbling manner of telling a story, I stopped in the middle of my sentence to try to explain to Bonnie how, bringing light to the world, she reminded me of a lighthouse–except that I took a shortcut after part of the sentence and simply held up one of the pillows. With her usual flair and delivery, she rolled her eyes and stated flatly, "Oh. So, I'm a pillow!"

I have never heard her or her parents laugh so hard.

About four days later, I received one of Bonnie's beautiful, hand-written notes that she loved to write on the many types of stationery that she owned. I still have it, of course, and would like to share with you a few sentences (I've left her smiley-faces exactly where she placed them).

> "... I am humbled and honored to hear that I am one of your lighthouses and it renews my strength to hear that God is using my life and situation for His purposes. ☺ I always think how unlikely it would have been for our paths to ever cross, except that somehow God pointed this guy named Tom in my direction and gave him the courage to sign up to Bonnie-sit. ☺ And to think of all that has transpired since; truly outstanding☺. All in all, it was a great evening of laughter and talking ... it was well worth every bit of energy spent! ... I hope you will always remember how special you and Kimberly are to me☺. God is good and to Him be all glory. ☺"

Since Bonnie's earthly body is gone and yet, she's practicing her ballet again, the question is, how will her earthly example affect my thoughts and actions from today forward?

I hope that reading the Bonnie Code will positively affect yours.

"For you see your calling, brethren, that not many wise according to the flesh, not many mighty, not many noble, are called. But God has chosen the foolish things of the world to put to shame the wise, and God has chosen the weak things of the world to put to shame the things which are mighty."
1 Corinthians 1:26–27 (New King James Version)

Tom and Bonnie–Christmas 2014

Bonnie's Locket—Including the unfolded note that she kept inside

MITOCHONDRIAL DISEASE RESOURCES

Australian Mitochondrial Disease Foundation, http://www. AMDF.org.au.

Codier, David and Estelle Codier. "Long-Term Central IV Access in Patients with Mitochondrial Disease." British Journal of Nursing 23, sup8 (2014). https://www.magonlinelibrary.com/ doi/abs/10.12968/bjon.2014.23.Sup8.S18

Codier, David and Estelle Codier. "Understanding Mitochondrial Disease and Goals for its Treatment." British Journal of Nursing 23, no. 5 (2014). https://www.magonlinelibrary.com/doi/ abs/10.12968/bjon.2014.23.5.254

"The Magic Bracelet Movie." https://www.youtube.com/ watch?v=GJSGPI3wvVI.

"Mitochondrial Disease." TheScientist. https://www.the scientist. com/search?for=mitochondrial%20disease

Mitochondrial Disease News. http://www.mitochondrialdisease-news.com.

"Mitochondrial Disease." National Institute of Neurological Disorders and Stroke. https://search.usa.gov/search?ut-f8=%E2%9C%93&affiliate=ninds&query=mitochondri-al+disease. Includes description of Nuclear DNA (nDNA) vs Mitochondrial DNA (mtDNA), the differences, and how Mito is inherited, among other excellent resources.

"This is MITO." Saratoga Film Academy. https://www.youtube.com/watch?v=qlnYbCxwnTk

The United Mitochondrial Disease Foundation. 1-888-317-8633. http://www.UMDF.org.

Vanderspuy, Martine. *A Little Book About MiTO*. Australian Mitochondrial Disease Foundation, 2017.

RECENT MITOCHONDRIAL DISEASE NEWS HEADLINES

Carvalho, Joana, PhD. "New Mouse Model May Advance Understanding of Mitochondria Protein Production and Dysfunction, Researchers Say." Mitochondrial Disease News (December 6, 2019). https://mitochondrialdiseasenews.com/2019/12/06/scientists-create-model-to-study-production-mitochondrial-proteins/.

Carvalho, Joana, PhD. "Women With Mitochondrial Disease More Prone to Pregnancy Complications, Study Shows." Mitochondrial Disease News (August 10, 2018). https://mitochondrialdiseasenews.com/2018/08/10/women-with-mitochondrial-disease-dysfunction-more-prone-to-pregnancy-complications/.

Chapman, Mary. "Nonprofits RARE Courage, All Wheels Up Partner on Survey Seeking to Improve Air Travel for Wheelchair Users." Mitochondrial Disease News (January 30, 2020). https://mitochondrialdiseasenews.com/2020/01/30/rare-courage-survey-air-travel-wheelchair/.

Inacio, Patricia, PhD. "Hotspot Therapeutics Secures $45M to Advance Drug Discovery Platform." Mitochondrial Disease News (July 20, 2018). https://mitochondrialdiseasenews.com/2018/07/20/

hotspot-therapeutics-secures-45m-advance-drug-discovery-platform/.

Inacio, Patricia, PhD. "NV354, Potential Therapy for Mitochondrial Diseases, Shows Promise in Preclinical Studies." Mitochondrial Disease News (October 19, 2018). https://mitochondrialdiseasenews.com/2018/10/19/potential-mitochondrial-disease-therapy-nv354-shows-promise-preclinical-studies/.

Lopes, Marques, PhD. "Clinicians Should Consider Different Wording in Cases of Unconfirmed Mitochondrial Disease, Study Suggests." Mitochondrial Disease News (April 12, 2019). https://mitochondrialdiseasenews.com/2019/04/12/different-terminology-used-unconfirmed-mitochondrial-disease-diagnosis/.

Luxner, Larry. "#NORD Summit – More than 700 Expected to Attend Oct 15-16 Rare Disease Summit in Washington." Sanfilippo News (September 21, 2018). https://sanfilipponews.com/2018/09/21/nordsummit-700-expected-attend-oct-15-16-rare-disease-summit-washington/.

Luxner, Larry. "US 'Right To Try' Law Meets With Mix of Praise and Criticism, Including Among Those With Rare Diseases." Mitochondrial Disease News (June 4, 2018). https://mitochondrialdiseasenews.com/2018/06/04/us-right-to-try-law-meets-with-mix-of-praise-and-criticism-including-among-those-with-rare-diseases/.

ENDNOTES

1 The United Mitochondrial Disease Foundation. http://www. UMDF.org, www.UMDF.org/au.

2 The United Mitochondrial Disease Foundation. http://www. UMDF.org, www.UMDF.org/au.

3 Vanderspuy, Martine. *A Little Book About MiTO*. Australian Mitochondrial Disease Foundation, 2017.

4 APGAR scores – Developed by Virginia Apgar in 1952, a New York anesthesiologist, to quantify the effects of obstetric anesthesia on babies. The test checks a babies' heart rate, muscle tone, and other signs to see if extra medical care or emergency care is needed. Test is usually performed twice on a newborn–once at one minute and once at five minutes after birth. Wikipedia, www.Kidshealth.org.

5 David Hallberg; American Ballet Theater; Wikipedia

6 *Websters New World Dictionary*, c1961, Introduction; Household Information Section

7 *Websters New World Dictionary,* c1961, Introduction

8 www.faithfacts.org

9 Holy Bible, New Living Translation (NLT)

10 *Life Application Study Bible*; James Chapter 2 Commentary

11 Gabriel, Charles Hutchinson. "I Stand Amazed in the Presence." WWW.hymnal.net. Side note: Such beautiful comments on these lyrics on the website, from Nigeria, Ghana, Fiji, and the US.

12 Quoted from Charles Dickens; *A Tale of Two Cities*

13 Duin, Steve. "The Gift." Wake Forest Magazine (June 25, 2011). Also, Poovey, Cherin. "Inside Pitch." (January 26, 2015).

14 Holy Bible; Habakkuk 1:12–14

15 Holy Bible; Habakkuk 2:9, 12, 15, 19

16 Holy Bible; Habakkuk 2:18–20

17 Holy Bible; Habakkuk Chapter 3

18 Michael Ward, University of Oxford Professor, at Hillsdale College Commencement, May 2015

19 John MacArthur, New Testament Commentary on Hebrews, page 104

20 Holy Bible; Matthew 22:37–39, Mark 12:29–31, Luke 10:27, Deuteronomy 6:5

21 www.harvest.org.

CPSIA information can be obtained
at www.ICGtesting.com
Printed in the USA
LVHW011723060221
678582LV00023B/1179